Voces Latinas

**Hispanic Adults
Speak to
Hispanic Young People**

Beth Johnson

TP THE TOWNSEND LIBRARY

Voces Latinas
Hispanic Adults Speak to
Hispanic Young People

TP THE TOWNSEND LIBRARY

For more titles in the Townsend Library,
visit our website: www.townsendpress.com

Photo credits:
Andres Idarraga courtesy Brown University/John Abromowski
Maria Cárdenas courtesy of Marc Beaudin
Lupe Valdez courtesy Dallas County Sheriff's Department
Rosie Molinary courtesy Rosie Molinary
Felipe Gutierrez courtesy Scripps Mercy Hospital, San Diego
All other photographs by Beth Johnson

Townsend Press, Inc.
439 Kelley Drive
West Berlin, New Jersey 08091
permissions@townsendpress.com

ISBN-13: 978-1-59194-225-2
ISBN-10: 1-59194-225-X

Library of Congress Control Number:
2010924210

CONTENTS

Introduction

It's an exciting time to be a Hispanic person in the United States. Hispanics are rapidly establishing themselves as a major economic, cultural, and political power in the U.S. The population figures speak for themselves: In the year 2000, 31 percent of U.S. residents were Hispanic. By 2009, that percentage had increased to 34 percent. Today, nearly one in six residents of this country, or nearly 50 million people, are Hispanic.

Those numbers will only increase. The Hispanic population of the U.S. is young, with a median age of 27.7 years (the median age for U.S. residents in general is 36.8 years). As this huge group has children, buys houses, goes to college, votes, shops for consumer goods, and so on, their numbers will have an enormous impact on the economic, cultural, and political development of this country.

That impact is already being felt. In 2009, Sonia Sotomayor, a Nuyorican, became the first Hispanic member of the U.S. Supreme Court. The Spanish-language TV network Univision has local stations in more than 50 U.S. cities. Hispanic voters' overwhelming support for Barack Obama helped ensure his victory in the 2008 presidential election. The number of Hispanic business leaders steadily grows. That group includes leaders such as Jim Padilla, former president and chief operating officer of Ford Motor Company, and Patricia Elizondo, senior vice president of Xerox Corporation. Monica Garcia serves as president of the Board of Education of the Los Angeles Unified School District, and Dr. France Córdova is president of Purdue University.

Despite successes such as these, challenges still lie ahead for Hispanic Americans. While the percentage of young Hispanics graduating from high school and attending college is rising, it still lags far behind corresponding percentages for Anglos. Too many Hispanics still live in *barrios*, pockets of poverty with dangerous streets and substandard schools. Gangs, drug use, and crime pull too many young people into what might initially look like *la vida loca*; however, this lifestyle leads to prison, despair, and death. Young Hispanics may find themselves caught between the cultural expectations of their parents, and the demands of the world outside their home.

To explore some of the challenges and rewards, the struggles and the triumphs, of being Hispanic in

Introduction

today's United States, we have invited ten remarkable men and women to share their stories in this book. They include people now living in Pennsylvania, Texas, California, Florida, New Jersey, and Connecticut. Their family roots can be traced to Puerto Rico, Mexico, and Colombia. The men and women include a professor, a college administrator, several businesspeople, a nurse, a sheriff, a law student, a teacher, and a writer. Their backgrounds include migrant work, prison, single parenthood, and struggles with addiction, racism, and sexism. As diverse as their experiences are, the people who tell their stories in this book share a common interest in reaching out an encouraging hand to young Hispanics growing up in this rapidly changing country we all call home.

Bienvenidos—enjoy their stories!

Paula González

About Paula González

At the age of 16, Paula González was a high-school dropout and a mother. Faced with the choice between a future of welfare dependence or an unhappy marriage, she took the unusual step of joining the New York City Painters' Union. Over the next fifteen years, she became an expert craftsperson, participating in a variety of projects, including the restoration of New York's Carnegie Hall. At age 37, Paula started taking classes at Brooklyn's Kingsborough Community College, and eventually she earned a degree in sociology at Brooklyn College. As a sociology student, she began reading books about teen pregnancy, welfare reform, Puerto Rican gender roles, and other topics that she had experienced firsthand. Her studies gave her a deepened perspective on her life and the lives of people around her. After the terrorist attacks of September 11, 2001, Paula left New York to live in Allentown, Pennsylvania. In Pennsylvania she completed her master's degree in social work at Temple University, where she is employed now as a program coordinator.

Voces Latinas

Paula González Speaks

I'm a Puerto Rican woman born and raised in the ghettos of Brooklyn, in New York City. I was the youngest of my mother's five children and the most rebellious of the girls. See, I was becoming too Americanized. My mother was raising her girls to be good Puerto Rican wives and mothers. School was not real important in my family, and after the eighth grade nobody cared if I dropped out—as long as I then stayed home doing laundry and other "women's work." I was taught to do everything in a house: cook, wash clothes by hand, sew, scrub a floor, paint, even fix the plumbing. I was taught that if it was in the house, it was "housework"—and it was my job.

The problem was that I didn't follow the house rules. I stopped going to school when I was 14, but I didn't tell my mother and I didn't stay home. I hung out on the street with all the other dysfunctional kids. Actually, there were things about school that I really liked. I was a "good" student in the sense that I was quiet and I listened. I loved science and history. As long as I could just listen to the teacher, I could absorb a lot. What I couldn't do was read or write—not well. Naturally, as I got older, it got harder to hide that fact.

Paula González

When I started high school, I had classes that involved a lot of lectures. I couldn't keep up, because I couldn't spell or write fast enough to take notes. When a teacher would ask me to read in class, I'd put on an act as though I was the coolest, freshest kid in class. I'd say, "What, yo? Me? You're calling on *me*? You think *I'm* gonna read this?" If I had to, I'd create some drama and storm out of class rather than admit I couldn't read.

At home there was no encouragement to do well in school. In fact, it was the opposite. Many times I heard "Reading too much makes you crazy." I think what that really meant was that reading gave you ideas, and ideas were dangerous. Ideas could make you think things that were different from what the group thought. Ideas could make you think you could go further than the group. And staying within the group was very, very important.

The group was the extended family. That was our world. We were taught to distrust and fear everyone else. Most of all we distrusted "them"—the white world out there. By the time I was 14, our family had moved twenty-seven times. We rented by the week, not just because that was all we could afford; weekly rentals also kept anyone from knowing us, kept the neighbors from getting curious about us, kept us girls from forming ties with anyone who might notice what was going on in our home.

My father was physically, sexually, and emotionally abusive. He was a barber who changed places of employment almost as often as we moved. I like to say that he was the richest poor man I've ever known. We catered to him as if he were a king. He ate separately from the rest of us, and we had to cool his food so it did not burn his mouth. At night we drew his bath and laid out his underwear and slippers in the bathroom. If anything was not to his liking—from the volume of the TV to the food we prepared—it had to be corrected immediately. Once when I was 13 and he was angry about something, he went outside and began nailing the doors shut. He told us he would set the place on fire and no one would be able to reach us until it was too late. People say, "He must have been crazy." No, he wasn't crazy. If he had been crazy, he would have nailed himself in the house with us. If he had been crazy, he would have hit a man bigger than he was, not a child. He wasn't crazy. He was abusive to the point that he had to control our very souls.

So by the time I was 14, I had stopped going to school and was staying away from home as much as possible. I worked the weekends as a candy girl in the Marcy Theatre on Broadway, in Brooklyn. One night my friends were going to a house party, but I got in from work too late and they left me. I didn't want to go home. So I found another party, and that is where I met Christobal González (my maiden name is also González). Oh my, he was so fine. He was tall and cute, with his hair cut in a Caesar, and he was dressed sharp. He asked me to dance, and we slow danced for hours. At the end of the night, he walked me home. When he asked if he could see me again, I said yes.

The first time he picked me up with his customized Chevy Camaro, my friends were going crazy. His car had a leather rooftop with a diamond-shaped window in the back. I felt like the luckiest girl around, and all my friends agreed. My man was fine, he had a car, and he had a job. He told me he was 18, but I found out about a month later that he was really 26. By this time, I didn't care how old he was; I was in love. I was able to talk to him about everything. I told him every secret I had, and he seemed understanding and sensitive.

When my mother found out that I was seeing him, she was afraid I'd become sexually active and disgrace her. Never mind that I was being sexually abused at home. She ordered me to either break it off or marry him. She told my father that if he didn't agree to let me get married, I was going to run away. Within a couple of weeks, Christobal asked my father for my hand in marriage, and my father gave it to him. I was too young to marry legally, so my mother went to court and got some sort of exemption for me.

Christobal wasn't so nice after my father gave me to him, and I didn't feel so lucky anymore. I was no longer allowed to do anything without asking my fiancé for permission. But I didn't fight it; both of my married sisters seemed pretty happy, and at last it seemed I was going to be a good Puerto Rican woman. I got busy preparing for the wedding. Christobal borrowed money from his brother-in-law, and we invited all of our friends. When we married, I was 15 and had known him for eight months. For my honeymoon, he took me to the Golden Gate Inn in Sheepshead Bay, Brooklyn, for one night.

After that, we went to live in the back of his mother's basement apartment. But I didn't care. I had my fine man, and everyone was still calling me lucky. I wanted to have a baby right away, and at 16 I had Christobal Jr. Oh my God, I was in love. He was such a pretty baby. But I didn't know how to take care of him and he cried a lot, and my husband wouldn't help.

He started drinking and smoking weed every day. He was always losing his job, and we hadn't gotten out of the basement. And now I was 17 and pregnant with my second son, Kenny. I was living with my two boys in a basement with an alcoholic drug addict who was unemployed most of the time. Meanwhile, I was doing the things I thought would make me a good wife and mother. I made my husband's shirts by hand. I starched his underwear.

Things got worse. Christobal humiliated me in public. He spit on me. And he forced me, again and again, to have sex against my will. When I went to my family and to my friends to tell them I was being raped, asking them to help me, they just stared at me. They told me what I was saying was impossible. They said that as a man's wife, it was my job to have sex with him whenever and however he wanted. They said because he was my husband, it could not be rape.

This is something I have trouble talking about even now, so many years later. Right now, thinking about it, I am shaking and feel sick to my stomach. When I began telling this story, I did not plan to talk about this part. It seemed too personal, and I didn't want to feel again the shame and guilt and confusion I had lived with. But then I remembered what it did to me when

I tried to find someone to listen and instead was told, "No, it's impossible; no, you're crazy; no, you're just making trouble; shut up, shut up, shut up, be quiet about it." I began to think that maybe what happened to me is happening to some young girl reading this story. Maybe, like me, she has no one to validate what she's experiencing. Maybe, even though she knows in her very soul what is happening, she is being told, "You are wrong."

So if you are that girl, I am telling you now: *You are not wrong.* Just because a guy is your boyfriend, or even your husband, he does not own your body. Just because you have had sex with him before does not mean you have given up your right to say no. Forcing someone to have sex against her will is rape. And rape is a crime, no matter who does it.

I looked for a way out. I had quit school at 14. I had no job skills. I could barely read. I tried to leave Christobal and go on welfare when I was 16, but the welfare office told me I had to go back to my parents until I was 18. I returned to the basement apartment for more abuse. This went on for two years, until I was 18. I knew nothing about any resources that could have helped me. I'd never heard of a domestic violence shelter. When I finally left, I stayed alone for only one

14

year. I was so lonely. Most of my friends were still single, and my sisters had their husbands and children. I met another older man, Angel, who also seemed very kind in the beginning, and at 20 I had Ivy, my daughter. I left Angel when Ivy was eight months old; I'd found out he was having an affair at work that had started when I was pregnant.

I was now 21 with three kids from two different men who didn't want to take care of them. It didn't matter if I took them to court: Christobal wouldn't work, and Angel offered me five dollars a week. My family wouldn't help either. So I was left on my own to care for my kids. I was scared all the time. I was afraid of losing my apartment. I was afraid of losing my kids. I was afraid I would die and leave them alone. And they could tell I was afraid. Christobal Jr. would rub my head when I cried. I loved them more than anything or anyone else in this world. But they needed and deserved to have a mother who could provide for them and keep them safe. They deserved a mother who was old enough and mature enough to make life decisions for them. Instead, they had me.

My kids went through a lot of hardship and a lot of emotional pain. Everything that happened to me happened to them, too. That's something you don't think about when you imagine having a baby. Nothing happens just to you anymore. It all happens to your kids. And when you're young and alone, a lot of bad things happen.

Along the way I met many young Puerto Rican girls just like me, and they all had dreams. We would stay up all night talking about the things we wanted for ourselves and our children. We talked about having our own apartment that wouldn't be taken away from us, maybe even a little house. We talked about having a husband who loved us and would accept our children from other men.

These girls were my closest friends. But when I began taking steps to make my dreams a reality, something very strange happened: I lost most of those friends. When I got off welfare and got my first real job, my friend Mary sent her daughter to return my house keys and to get hers. She imagined that I thought I was better than she was because I was working. I was so hurt. I had thought she was my best friend. She told everyone that I was stupid for going to work and leaving my kids with a sitter. Mary told me that no man was going to want me, that a good Puerto Rican woman takes care of her kids and her house.

Rejections like that happened again and again

as I took steps to become independent. Just like my parents, the group did not want me going "out there" into the larger world. The message was "If you think *we* treat you badly, you can only imagine how *they* will treat you." I'd grown up hearing so many horror stories about "them." But as I looked ahead to a life where every day was the same as the one before it, I began to think, "But my own people lied about so much. Maybe they're lying about this, too."

I knew that I could not live the life that my mother had planned for me.

When I looked near me for women who could guide me in another direction, there were none. I had to look further, to find women outside of my family who could help me. These women, who were all older than I was, helped me understand that it was possible for a woman to have a good life that was not filled with abuse. One of the first women who helped me was Lucy Quilles. She was a Jehovah's Witness who came to my door one day. I was 19, and she was about 30. Like me, she had had her children very young. But she seemed to have it all together. She drove her own car! She had traveled! She was pretty and well-dressed, and her children did well in school and seemed happy. Lucy taught me how to read well enough to get my GED.

She came over at least once a week during the day and read along with me. She did this for about two years. In the meantime, I went to beauty school and worked as a beautician for three years. That is a very hard life. Beauticians basically make their money working three twelve-hour days—Thursday, Friday, and Saturday. If you can't work those hours, you can't do well. And I wasn't a very good beautician, so my tips were lousy.

I knew I had to do something else to support myself and the children. The trade unions in New York were just opening up to women, so at age 23 I joined the painters' union, and I worked as a painter for the next fifteen years. I liked the work and made good money, but eventually I became sensitive to the chemicals I was working with and had to stop. When I decided to go to college, everyone again thought I had gone crazy. The first day I drove myself to college, I cried all the way. I could hear my mother's voice in my head saying, "There she goes again, always wanting to be different." Even my son Christobal told me I was too old and it didn't make sense. But I made it all the way to my master's degree with a grade point average of 3.87. I graduated with honors.

Today my kids are all grown up. They're all right, but they grew up without a father, and with a mother that was always struggling to give them the things they deserved. I was there, but I was always worrying, always scared. Even today it is hard for me not to cry when I think of what they went through.

When I see my little sisters pushing their baby carriages, I know how much they love those babies, and I know how hard their lives can be. For those that are thinking of having a baby, I can only say I wish you would wait a little longer, until you're older and have more opportunities and more skills to care for a child. Because love is not enough—really, it's not. And if your boyfriend, friends, and family members say they'll be there, remember that help comes with a price. People who are helping you will feel that they have the right to tell you how to raise your kids and how to run your life. And people move on, even fathers. If you already have children, don't be scared of doing things differently. Dream big for yourself and your babies. But don't only dream. Do the hard work to make your dreams come true.

We all grow up thinking that the way our family or our community does things is the right way, the normal way. That's natural; kids learn what they live with. And fortunately, for many people, their families and communities are sources of love and encouragement.

What I want you to take away from my story is this: If the things the people close to you are telling you seem wrong, maybe they *are* wrong. And if you're being told, "But that's how things are, because we're Puerto Rican"—or Mexican, or Dominican, or African American, or Jamaican, or French, or Chinese, or Martian, or whatever—well, I hope you'll question that. Many of the things that happened in my life weren't okay, no matter what anybody said. I knew that. But with so many people telling me, "You're wrong," it took me many years to trust my own judgment. I wish you the strength and wisdom to trust yours.

Angel Figueroa

About Angel Figueroa

People who don't know Angel Figueroa might well look at him and think, "He's got it made." This Reading, Pennsylvania, businessman is looked up to in his community. He's a college graduate. He has a wife, children, and a house in the suburbs. But Angel's journey has taken him through some of the darkest corners of the human experience. He speaks openly about those dark places and their contrast with his life today.

Angel Figueroa Speaks

Here are two assumptions many people make:

> If you're white, middle class, and live in the suburbs, you'll go to college.
>
> If you're a poor Latino growing up in Jersey City, New Jersey, you'll end up dead, locked up, or running the freakin' streets.

I know all about that second assumption. My goal in life is to change it.

My parents came from Puerto Rico. I was born and raised in Jersey City, and lived there until I was 17. I dropped out of high school. My mom was single when she had me at 14. She and my dad eventually had six kids. Dad worked in a factory in New York City's garment district. Everybody assumed I'd work in a factory, too.

Instead, I'm living in the beautiful town of Reading, Pennsylvania, where I became the first Hispanic member of the city council. I've run for mayor of the city. I'm vice president of an organization that trains community leaders. I'm a college graduate, and I'm working on my master's degree in business administration. I'm married to a beautiful woman who is a college graduate and a nurse. My little daughters play in a grassy yard with trees all around.

It hasn't been a straight shot to get here. I'm very lucky to be alive at all. I hope you can learn something from my journey. I want you to realize that if you avoid the mistakes I made, you can progress further than I have. You really can. You don't have to accept others' assumptions about your life.

My upbringing was very typical for our Latino neighborhood in Jersey City. Dad worked; Mom stayed home and took care of the kids. I remember spending a lot of hot summer days just sitting on somebody's stoop waiting for the next thing to happen. We ran up and down the block, sneaking into people's yards to shinny up their trees and steal peaches or cherries. We had a lot of fun. We had enough food, and new clothes when school started, because my dad always worked. I had no idea we were poor until somebody told me.

Another way we were typical was that my father never picked up a ball and bat and played with me, or sat down to talk with me about the dos and don'ts of life. I love my dad very much and appreciate all he did for me. He worked hard to provide for his family. In his experience, that's what a father's job was. But talking with us, passing on life lessons—no, there was none of that. I don't think he understood the importance of playing that role in his children's life. He was very *machista*. Looking back, I wonder if things might have been different if my dad had been a more active presence in my life.

My mother—all my friends wanted a mom like her. She was the cool mom. For her, being a parent meant being your friend. When I was 13, she was taking me along to parties where people thought it was cute if I chugged a Budweiser. It was cool with her if I came home at 3:00 a.m. Again, I love my mom, and she's very important to me. But she did things for us that I would never do for my children today.

As for school, I did pretty well. I was a bright kid. And my parents cared about school to the extent that they made sure I went and they asked if I'd done my homework. But nobody ever said, "Hey, you need to graduate from high school. You should go to college." I had a lot of cousins, older guys who were constantly in and out of our house, and I observed that if you were a man, you left school and you worked.

My day came. The summer I turned 14, my dad said, "You're coming to work in the factory." I said I didn't want to do factory work. He said, "So find something else. You've got two weeks." I went to the mall and walked into the athletic department of the J.C. Penney store. I thought maybe I could get a discount on sneakers if I worked there. I talked to a white guy named Tom. He had me fill out an application and said, "I'd like you to come back, but when you do, wear a tie." I went home all excited, saying, "Mom! Dad! I'm going to work at the mall! But I have to wear a tie." Well, that caused a family crisis. No one in my family knew how to tie a tie. My dad was really stressing about it. But Mom went to a department store and bought a brown clip-on tie. I proceeded to wear that tie to work every day for the next two and a half weeks. Finally Tom said, "You know, you could wear a different tie once in a while." I was embarrassed, but I said, "I don't know how to put a tie on." And God bless him, Tom took me aside and taught me how to tie a tie.

That incident might not have meant anything to most people. But it meant a lot to me. It helped me realize I really *could* do more than factory work. I could be part of this larger, different society. And there would be good people like Tom along the way to show me the ropes, if I'd let them.

It was that same summer that another important incident happened. You know how in a big family, there's always one person you especially look up to? For me it was a particular uncle. And he really was cool—a smart guy. He'd graduated from one of the top high schools in Jersey City. But he lived with his mom in a family of seven; he had to pay rent, and instead of going on to college, he went out to hustle. So one day when I was sitting around with him, he pulled out a joint and said, "You want some?"

I sometimes wonder what would have happened if I'd said no that day. Would it have made any difference? He was my cool uncle—good-looking, well built—my role model. If my dad and I had had a more active relationship, if he'd talked to me about making decisions, maybe I would have thought about the possible consequences of my uncle's offer. But my dad and I never would have talked about anything like that. Never.

But I didn't say no; I said yes. And you know, I didn't smoke again until the next summer. But once I started, it wasn't just weed. I got into LSD and the other trip drugs. Man, I thought I was living life, when all I was doing was playing with death. Teenage males—they think they're immortal. I saw two of my buddies OD. But I never thought, "That could be me." I didn't see the seeds of destruction I was sowing in my own life. And there was nobody—none of my so-called friends—who ever said, "Hey, you better slow down," because they were too busy messing up their own lives.

Things picked up with blinding speed. I began selling weed for my uncle, and I got caught in a school zone with thirty-five bags. I was arrested and sentenced to a six-month outpatient program, which was cool with me, because I got to spend my time with other druggies. School started in the fall and officially I went back, but really, my summer never ended. I was hanging out full time—drinking, smoking, you name it. I missed about sixty-five days that year. I had to make money to support my habit, so I became the go-to guy for mescaline and acid. Mom tried to get a grip on me. She put me into a court-ordered thirty-day rehab. I came out having met Alison, a white girl from the 'burbs. Her father was an architect. She was into a whole different level of drugs. I began doing heroin, and everything really went to hell.

I think it's fortunate, ultimately, that my plunge into addiction happened so intensely and so fast. If it hadn't been that way, I don't think I'd be alive today. Overnight, I was doing $200 a day. I wasn't injecting; I was snorting. So in order to chase that dragon, I had to constantly do more and more and more. It all seems like a nightmare now. I'd disappear for three or four days up in Spanish Harlem, lost with the other junkies. Thank God that even though I was out there, I maintained a pretty clean body. The depths that human beings can sink to—it's difficult to even think of that now. One night I was on 110th Street and 2nd Avenue at 3:00 in the morning with some dealers. Along came this woman who said, "I need crack. I don't have any money, but I'll do anything." One of the guys said, "You have to do all of us." There were six of us. She had a room. We all went up there. The first guy went in, did what he did, and came out. Then the next guy, and the next. I was the sixth. The moment I went into that room with her, I puked my brains out. It was so sick, so sad and terrible.

Back home, I started going through withdrawal. My mom would hold me so tight, like a baby, trying to help me through it. Then I'd start crying and manipulate her into letting me go, and I'd leave and get high. I'd dropped out of school by then. I was hardly even a human being. My dad—he was so hurt. He couldn't look at me.

Finally, the fall after I'd turned 17, my mother said, "I can't deal with you no more. I got other kids to raise; you gotta go." She arranged to get me into a long-term residential program in Pennsylvania called Hogar Crea. Hogar Crea originated in Puerto Rico, and in my opinion, it's a great program. They don't "rehab" you; they re-educate you. Take a chair, for example. If a leg breaks and you just fix the leg, that's rehab. But if you take the chair completely apart and re-build it, that's re-education. That's what they did for me at Hogar Crea.

When I arrived and they put me into detox, I weighed eighty-six pounds. And I still didn't think I had a drug problem. I still thought of what was going on as a phase, just a time I was going through.

Hogar taught me . . . everything. I learned about

honesty, integrity, compassion, character. The other residents, they were *compañeros*, a brotherhood. I learned; I relapsed; I fell; they confronted me and worked with me and changed my life. I met such incredible people. There was one guy—Santiago—who had been a heroin addict for thirty years. He had AIDS, and he died there in Hogar. He was the oldest resident, and I was the youngest. We were *el viejo* and *el bebe*. We talked a lot. Santiago told me, "You don't have to be like me. In life, be a 'noble thief.' Take the good from the people you meet, and leave the bad behind."

In Hogar, I found my voice as a community activist. I got involved in civic responsibility and working for change. At one point, when I was helping to organize an anti-drug march, I met Isamac, the girl who would become my wife. She was president of an organization called SOLA out of Millersville University, where she was a student. You have to understand that I had never in my life met a Puerto Rican female who was in college. I fell in love with her immediately—first with her beauty, but then with her intellect, with her drive to get more out of life. But I was still in treatment and not allowed to have a girlfriend, even if she would have had me. So we became friends and stayed in touch while we focused on what we each needed to do.

When I got out of Hogar, I still felt too weak to cope with returning to Jersey City. So I stayed in the beautiful quaint town of Lancaster, Pennsylvania, determined to rebuild my life there. I was turned away by many, many employers because of my lack of a high-school diploma. But another good man came into my life—a tall, skinny white guy named Pete, who ran a shoe store. I went in for an application, and I think he could see I was a little desperate for work. He interviewed me on the spot—not a formal job interview; he just talked to me as a human being. He gave me the job, and I stayed with him for three years, eventually becoming assistant store manager.

But I wanted more. I attended a six-month GED prep class at the adult literacy council and passed the test. At the age of 23, I started my own advertising business. Then Isamac decided to move to Reading to pursue her nursing degree. I understood it was what she needed to do, but oh my God, it was depressing. Then I thought, "Well, maybe this is an opportunity," and I went into the military. I joined the Army National Guard for six years. The military was a very therapeutic environment for me, a little like what I'd had in Hogar Crea. The structure and regimentation were very good for me. If I'd gone into the military at a younger age, I would have made it my career.

When I came out of the military, Isamac and I were married. What she saw in me I will never know. When we met, I had nothing, absolutely nothing, to offer her. I was a high-school dropout who was just getting out of freaking rehab. Her family was terribly concerned. Her friends at college were horrified. But she saw something in me that to this day I don't fully understand. We've been together for fifteen years now and have built a beautiful life. She is the spine that goes up my back. She has always said, "We can do it," and together, we have.

I knew I wanted a college degree, and the GI bill gave me a way to get one. By taking community college and university classes at the same time, I completed my bachelor's degree in two years and three months. But getting started was very difficult. I enrolled in my first class, English Composition 101, and after three weeks the instructor pulled me aside and said, "I think you need ESL (English as a Second Language)." I didn't know what to say. She went on, "It seems to me that when you write, you're thinking in Spanish." But my first language is English! That was both embarrassing and discouraging, to the point that I withdrew from college for a while. But eventually I said to myself, "Okay, you left school during your sophomore year. You just don't know enough. So go back and learn what you never got." I enrolled in some very basic English courses to work on my skills. I learned that I could even earn a lot of professional credits for work I'd done in the past.

So in a short span of time I did several very different things: I started taking classes at Reading Area Community College and Albright College; I ran for and won my city council seat; and I went to work for iLEAD, a nonprofit organization that helps develop leadership in struggling communities. I'm deeply involved in local politics. I hope to someday go to law school and ultimately run for Congress. I want so much to change those assumptions I was talking about, to change the expectations for poor urban kids that no one expects much from. I think about this kid— Orlando—who I met when I was running for mayor. He was 16 and a junior at Reading High School. When we were talking, I said, "Hey, Orlando, where are you going to college?" He gave me a sort of dazed look and said, "No one has ever asked me that before." And that just tears me up inside. *Why* hadn't anyone ever asked him? Why didn't anyone ask me? Why do people just assume that a poor inner-city Latino wouldn't be interested in college? I will spend the rest of my days working to see that kids—all kinds of kids—realize that they have choices in life.

When I look back on the bad times—and they were very bad—I realize that the flip side of it all is that those bad times gave me such a hunger to do more in life. I nearly threw it all away. When I was 24 and entered politics, there were people who were quick to say, "Oh, Angel—he was a junkie in Jersey City." But I was quicker: I went to the newspapers and put the whole story out there. And you know what? People respected me for it. They came up and said, "We're glad to have someone who understands what's going on in the cities." That's why I have no shame about my past. Yeah, maybe when I'm running for office some day I'll lose the support of some people who can't look beyond my past. But as I look at it, if the story of my journey can save one soul, that's worth so much more.

Guadalupe Quintanilla

About Guadalupe Quintanilla

Guadalupe Quintanilla was the first Hispanic woman to be an administrator at the University of Houston in Texas. Since joining the university's faculty forty years ago, she has served as assistant vice president for academic affairs, director of the Mexican-American studies program, and associate professor of modern languages. She has been a consultant to the Houston Police Department, for which she developed a nationally acclaimed cross-cultural communications program. She was nominated to be U.S. assistant attorney general, has served as a representative to the United Nations, and has spoken at countless conferences, both in the U.S. and abroad. But as you will learn when you read her essay, the most remarkable thing about "Lupita" Quintanilla is not where she is now, but how far she has traveled to get there.

Guadalupe Quintanilla Speaks

I dropped out of first grade when I was thirteen years old. Yes, you read that correctly. I was a thirteen-year-old first-grader, and I quit school.

How did such a thing happen? I will tell you. I was born in 1937 in Nogales, Mexico, just a few miles south of the Arizona border. When my parents separated, I went to live with my grandparents in a rural town deep in southern Mexico. There were no schools there. There weren't even any paved roads. Still, I learned a great deal. My grandparents ran a little store inside our house, and I helped out there. As a five-year-old, I would stand on a box to use the telephone and call in orders. Sometimes when the suppliers heard a child's voice, they would hang up, but some of the other suppliers became used to talking with me. I learned to read and write, and to work with numbers.

Then my grandfather began to lose his sight. We moved to Brownsville, Texas, in hopes that the doctors there could help him. Sadly, they could not, and he became completely blind.

In Brownsville, I was enrolled in school. And then the trouble began. Although I could read and write well, I could do those things only in Spanish. But I was given an IQ test—in English. I didn't understand any of the questions. I scored 64 points, which classified me as seriously mentally retarded. Although I was 12, I was put into first grade—in a class of six-year-olds. No one even tried to teach me. The teacher had me cut out pictures and take little kids to the bathroom. It was awful. I was bewildered by what was going on around me. Everyone was speaking a language I didn't understand. The other children teased me for being so stupid.

After four months, things came to a head. I was alone at recess, as usual, and a man cutting the grass greeted me. "*Buenas tardes*," he said. I was so excited to hear someone speak to me in Spanish, *la lengua de mi alma, la lengua de mi abuelita!* (The language of my soul, the language of my grandmother!) Eagerly I answered him. Like a flash, a teacher swooped down and grabbed me by the arm. She marched me to the principal's office, where she and the principal both shouted strange English words at me. To this day, I do not know why they were so angry. Was it something about this particular man? Was it simply that I was not supposed to speak Spanish at all? I'll never know.

What I do know is that I was humiliated more than I could bear. There was no force on earth that could make me go back to that place. I went home and told my family I was quitting school. And that is how I became a thirteen-year-old first-grade dropout.

I was very happy to be at home. I thought school was not essential for a girl. Nobody—least of all me—thought I should prepare to support myself. My grandparents, who were very loving and kind to me, were also very traditional. They raised me to be a good Hispanic wife and mother. My grandmother taught me to cook and clean and sew. I read novels and poetry and newspapers to my grandfather for hours. Everyone assumed that my life's job would be caring for a home and children.

My grandfather was getting older. He wanted to know that I would be protected after he was gone. In our world, "protected" meant "married." And so, at age 16, I married. My grandparents came to live with my husband and me. Within five years I had my three children—Victor, Mario, and Martha. My life was simple and happy. I took care of everyone—my husband, my children, and my grandparents. I could not have been more traditional. I would actually put my husband's shoes on his feet and tie the laces for him.

But my traditional upbringing had not prepared me for everything. As my children started school, I saw something bad happening. Victor, Mario, and Martha were as bright as they could be. They knew so many stories and songs and rhymes and prayers. They were quick-witted and funny. And yet, when they began bringing home report cards, their grades were poor.

They were put in a group called "Yellow Birds." I soon realized what "Yellow Birds" really meant; it was the label for "slow learners."

All my memories of my own school days came flooding back. I had been labeled "retarded." I had accepted the idea that school was not for me. But I could not accept that idea for my beautiful, bright children. I *knew* they were not "slow learners"!

I went to their school and talked to their teachers and principal. That was very difficult for me. People think that Hispanic parents do not care about education, because they are not likely to do things like call the teachers or join the PTA. In fact, the opposite is true. Most Hispanic parents have such great respect for education that they would never interfere with their child's schooling. They think, "She's *la maestra*; she must be right!" But I went. And the principal told me the truth. He said, "Your children are confused. They speak only Spanish at home. They don't know how to learn in English."

I realized the principal was right. Yes, in our Spanish-speaking home, it was clear that my children were very bright. But in an English-speaking school, they were lost—just as I had been lost in that first-grade classroom.

I knew what I had to do. In order to help my children succeed, I was going to have to learn English, and learn it well.

That was the beginning of a long, difficult journey for me. At that time in Brownsville, there were no English language programs for adults. I would have to find another way to learn. I went to the local high school to ask if I could sit in on some classes. But when the school administrators looked at my records, they saw the word "retarded." They told me, "You'd just be taking space in the classroom away from someone who could learn." I tried the local hospital, where I served as a volunteer. Could I sit in on their nursing classes? No, I was told—not without a high-school diploma. I got the same answer at Texas Southmost College and at the telephone company, where operators were being trained.

I was so discouraged. I walked home from the telephone company in the rain, crying, feeling like a complete failure. But somehow the next day, I woke up with fresh courage. I went back to the college and found a Spanish-speaking student. I asked him, "*Quién decide quién asiste a la escuela aquí?*" (Who decides who goes to school here?) He told me it was the registrar. I looked through the faculty parking lot until I found the spot marked RESERVED FOR REGISTRAR. I waited by that car for hours until a man came to get into it. Fortunately, he spoke Spanish. I told him that I *had* to attend classes in order to become educated and help my children. I don't think he had much hope for me. "You've never gone to school at all," he said. "How can you handle college classes?"

"Just let me try," I said.

Finally he agreed, and I tried. And it was terribly, terribly difficult. I got up at 4:00 a.m. to study. I had a long bus ride to school. At noon I hurried home to fix my husband's lunch. I'd rush back to class, then go home again to be there when my children returned from school. There were times I went to the ladies' room during break and cried. I would look at myself in the mirror and say, "What are you doing? Why don't you go home and watch *I Love Lucy* on TV?"

But I did it. Even today, I can hardly understand how. I believe it was the love for my children that motivated me. I made the dean's list that first semester. I began to think that I could do more than just learn English. I began to think that I, the first-grade dropout, the "retarded" girl, could earn a college degree.

I will not take the time to tell you the whole long story here. But I *did* earn my college degree. And then

I earned a master's degree, and then a doctoral degree in education. I joined the faculty of the University of Houston, where I still teach today. And my children, the "slow learners"? The oldest, Victor, is an attorney in San Antonio, Texas. He works in estate planning. The second, Mario, is an emergency room physician in Houston. And my youngest, Martha, is an attorney. She has just retired as chief of the Family Violence Division of the Dallas district attorney's office.

Now I would like to tell you not just about me, but about some of the things I have learned on my journey. They are things that I hope you, as young Latinas, will take to heart.

Let me start with a few lines by the great Mexican poet Amado Nervo. He wrote:

"Porque veo al final de mi rudo camino que yo fui el arquitecto de mi propio destino."
"When I got to the end of my long journey in life, I realized that I was the architect of my own destiny."

I insist that every student in every class I teach—whether it's Hispanic Women in Literature, Public Speaking in Spanish, or Latin Folklore of the Southwest—memorize those lines. They contain, in my opinion, the most important lesson a person can learn.

And that lesson is that your future lies in your own hands. You—and only you—are the architect of your own destiny.

I think that lesson is especially important, and in some ways especially difficult, for Hispanic women. Our world is changing rapidly, but for many of us, cultural expectations still carry a lot of weight. The traditional ways can be very comfortable. The closeness and support of the Latino family can be a very wonderful thing. But the flip side is that many of our young people find it hard to separate from the family and to learn to make independent decisions. Again and again, I see promising Latino students—both male and female—grow so homesick at the university that they drop out. I've heard "Our culture gives us strong roots, but we need to strengthen our wings." I think that is true.

In my own case, I met with a lot of resistance when I returned to school. My grandfather actually stopped speaking to me. To him, it was demeaning to the family to have a woman "on the street." He didn't mean like a streetwalker, but simply in the world outside of the home. He believed that by going "out there" I was neglecting my family. That was painful for me—to feel the disapproval of someone I loved and respected so much—but I had to stand firm for what I believed was right for me and my children. For women especially, trying to achieve that kind of independence is difficult. As we try to blossom in the Anglo world, we must respect the traditions of our parents. At the same time, we must recognize—and help *them* recognize—that sometimes those traditions can hold us back.

We may not even realize how our culture makes us out of sync with the larger society. Once when Mario and Victor were teenagers, they and another Latino boy were invited to a concert by an Anglo friend. They said they'd be home at 5:00 p.m. At 5:15, when they weren't back, the other Hispanic mom called me and asked if I'd heard anything. At 5:30 I called the Anglo boy's mom to ask if she knew why they were late. She was *so* angry with me! She said, "I have company! The boys know what they're doing!" and actually hung up on me. I was astonished! Why was she angry? I realized she thought I was ridiculously overprotective. And by her standards, I guess I was. But to me and the other Hispanic mom, it was perfectly normal.

From one perspective, that kind of protectiveness is simply loving. But we need to be aware of the downside. A fascinating study was done here in Houston about why many Latino children, in general, do not do as well in school as Anglo children. One thing that the study found is that most Latino children are less likely to ask questions. When they need help, they don't say so. I see that even at the university level. And I think part of the reason is that, in general, Latino children are accustomed to living in a supportive, protective family environment where they don't *have* to ask for much. Someone is always saying, "Do you need this? Would you like that? Can I help you?" As a result, these children, according to research, don't learn to speak up and ask for themselves. It's interesting, isn't it, that there is no word for "assertive" in Spanish? The closest is *agresivo*, and the meaning of that is quite different. To be assertive means to be clear about what you want. It means going after what you want. It does not mean being aggressive, or angry, or rude, or somehow unwomanly.

But assertiveness is not a value that our culture promotes. And that is our loss, because if you develop the ability to be assertive, there's no telling what you might accomplish. Let me tell you a story that illustrates what I mean. Some years back I was driving through a pretty neighborhood here in Houston. I thought, "When I retire, I'd like to live here." Later I saw a house in that neighborhood come up for sale. I called the real estate agent to ask about it. But he told me no, the house was not actually for sale. I said, "But there's a sign in the yard." He insisted no, there'd been some mistake, and it wasn't for sale.

Well, I thought about that for a while. I knew the house was for sale. Why would the agent tell me it wasn't? Hmm—could it be my Spanish accent? So I had Mario call. He has a Spanish name, of course, but he doesn't have an accent. And he was *Dr.* Quintanilla, the emergency room physician. Well, he got a different answer. The agent told Mario the house *was* for sale, but for a very high price. Then we had a friend of Mario's call. He is an Anglo, a police officer named Robert Jones. The agent told Robert Jones the house was for sale—and for *one-third the price* he had told Mario.

When Robert told me that, I said, "Buy the house, but have the contract made out to 'Robert Jones or his assignees'"—meaning that Robert could turn the house over to whomever he wanted. Of course, I was actually the buyer. When Mario and I went with Robert to the closing and the real estate agent realized who had really bought the house, he was so angry he would not even speak to us.

And you know what? Since that time, we have

bought six more houses in that neighborhood. When we own them all, we'll rename the street "Quintanilla Drive."

That's what being assertive can do for you. I say, "Don't get mad. Get ahead."

Other specific advice for young Latinas? I think of three things:

Get your degree before you marry.
Remember that no one can build *your* future
better than you can.
Realize the great importance of having choices
in your life.

Why wait to marry? As I stress to young women again and again, it's tremendously important to have the *freedom of choice in your life*. And I see how terribly difficult it is for my students to pursue their dreams when they are trying to juggle a marriage and children. In addition, when you are very young, it is unlikely that you have the maturity to look into the future and know what you're going to want in a year, or five years, or ten. I have never regretted my husband or children, but certainly it would have been wiser for me to have waited until I was older to marry.

And the other points are all tied together with the first. Once you earn a degree, you have the ability to support yourself; you have a choice. If you choose to stay home to care for your children, that's fine. But if you feel cooped up in the house because you have no ability to support yourself and have no belief in yourself—no, that is not fine; you are worthy of more.

I have shown you this line of poetry before. But I will leave it with you again as a message from a first-grade dropout, a "retarded" student, a young mother of three children who were being told they could not succeed:

"When I got to the end of my long journey in life, I realized that I was the architect of my own destiny."

Please, believe these words. They are true. Your own life, like mine, can be the proof.

Andres Idarraga

About Andres Idarraga

O f all the students at Yale Law School—perhaps the most respected law school in the country—Andres Idarraga stands out. This native of Medellin, Colombia, is an ex-felon. Before beginning his college career, Andres served more than six years in a federal penitentiary. In addition to the remarkable story he tells here, Idarraga has become an influential spokesman for voting rights for ex-convicts. When he realized that under existing Rhode Island law he would be unable to vote until he turned 58, he began fighting for ex-felons' right to vote upon their release from prison. He worked with a local voters' rights organization, successfully bringing about a change in the state law in November 2006. Idarraga registered to vote immediately.

Andres Idarraga Speaks

I n the spring of 2008, I graduated from Brown University in Rhode Island. On that special day, a friend gave me a card that perfectly summed up what my education means to me. The card included a quote from *Lives on the Boundary*, a book by Mike Rose, who overcame hardship on the streets of South L.A.

(Los Angeles) to become a respected educator. In his book, Rose describes the damage that can result from growing up in poverty. He writes: "It wasn't the violence of South L.A. that marked me, for sometimes you can shake that ugliness off. What finally affected me was subtler, more pervasive: *I cannot recall a young person who was lost in work or one old person who was passionate about a cause or idea.*"

What Rose is writing about is the sad result of being passive participants in our own lives, instead of active creators. Too many of us have lost the ability to "be passionate about a cause or idea." In this world of instant gratification, we have forgotten how to form long-term goals. We have forgotten how to define our dreams.

Many of you reading these words have traveled winding and difficult roads. Those roads—maybe leading through immigration, poverty, drugs, violence, and troubles with the law—will leave their marks on you. In spite of those marks, it is within your power to create a positive and fulfilling future. But first you must define what that future will be. Why is this important? Because, if *you* do not define your future, you'd better believe that your future will be defined *for* you. I'll say it again: If you do not take active control of your life, circumstances will control you, leading you to familiar dead ends. Do you know where others' definitions of you will place you? That's right—in poverty or in prison, or worse.

Let me tell you about my own winding road and how I finally learned to become the definer of my own destiny.

I was born in Colombia thirty-one years ago. My father was a factory worker. Soon after I was born, he caught what he called *la fiebre*—the fever to come to the U.S. He'd heard that in the U.S., a man willing to do backbreaking work could get ahead. He came to the States illegally and went to work in Rhode Island. When I was 7, he had legalized his status and he returned to Colombia for the rest of our family.

Four years later, my parents separated. My mother suddenly had two sons to support on her own—and not a great grasp of English. She was proud and didn't complain, but I could see that she was struggling, financially and otherwise. As I became a young man, it was hard for me to realize that I couldn't help her.

School had always come easily to me. I learned English quickly and did very well. Soon I was in Honors classes. By the time I was in tenth grade, I was in classes with all seniors. The school had nothing left to offer me. Then a guidance counselor persuaded a local college prep school, Moses Brown, to give me a scholarship.

Now things began to get dicey. The transfer to Moses Brown was total culture shock for me. The area I lived in was probably 50 percent Latino and 20 percent Black. But Moses Brown was almost all white, with maybe five Spanish students.

Besides that, ever since junior high I'd been hearing "You're bright; you're capable; you're the one who can make it out of here." And now I was at a college prep school. This was "out"; this was my destination. I was supposed to be thrilled. Instead, I felt that a judgment was being made about where I had come from. If this was the "good" place, then where I had come from must be "bad."

This is all with the benefit of hindsight. Back then, I probably couldn't have put what I was feeling into words. But something was off. In response, I didn't let myself get involved at Moses Brown. Instead, I hung around my old school as much as possible. I guess I was trying to prove that I still belonged there.

Money was still tight. My scholarship didn't cover lunch money. Mom had to come up with that. And then one day at my old school someone asked me to do an errand—a drug errand. He gave me $60. That was thirty days of lunch money. At that moment, $60 in my pocket meant a lot more to me than a Moses Brown education. It's hard to know the value of something you've never seen. My parents could talk about wanting *algo mejor* for me, but they couldn't explain what "something better" was. It's not like they could say, "You know that successful lawyer down the street? You could be like him." In my world, ideas like "a future," "an education," or "a profession," were myths, like a unicorn or Sasquatch.

Senior year came along. The guidance counselor began asking me about my college plans. It was as if he was drawing a line in the sand. Was my future going to be about college or about the streets? At that moment, the streets were more attractive. So I said no, I wouldn't be going to college. In fact, I decided to quit school completely. My mother begged me to at least get my high-school diploma. So I compromised by dropping out of Moses Brown and returning to my old high school. And now I was the one seeking out those errands.

I graduated from high school and became a full-time street kid and drug dealer. That was my life for two and half years—until I was arrested. Just after my twentieth birthday I began serving a fourteen-year sentence in a Rhode Island maximum-security state prison.

Going to prison was not that eye-opening of an experience for me. Sadly, in a lot of neighborhoods, maybe even in yours, it's considered part of the normal life cycle. I was nervous as hell going in, but almost immediately I began getting shout-outs from people I knew. "Hey, Andres! Heard you got busted—we've been waiting for you!" I began feeling pretty much at home. Soon I had no vision of myself outside that box.

For the first two years or so, I had my little routine. I'd spend my days lifting weights, playing cards, playing chess, and watching TV. Lifting weights was a big deal. I went in there at about 150 pounds. In a maximum-security place, you want to look like you can defend yourself. So I spent a lot of time at the gym, which was in the same building as the library.

As I passed the library, I'd hear the guys in there having amazing conversations about the news, books, economics, politics, business, philosophy, you name it. My first response was sarcastic. I thought, "Yeah, yeah; you come to prison, and suddenly you're smart guys." So I kept passing by and going to the gym. But when I'd be chilling in the yard, there those guys would be again, having really interesting talks. I began to chime in sometimes. They'd say, "Hey, why don't you come hang with us in the library?" I resisted. I didn't want to become one of those prison talkers.

But going into my third year, I was getting really bored. You can only lift so many weights. I began going into the library, and wow, the conversations were tremendous. People on the outside would be surprised at the wit and the depth of knowledge these guys have. In addition to talking with them, I began to read, and read, and read. I read biographies, like the one of Nelson Mandela, who spent twenty-seven years in prison and then became president of South Africa. I read about the life of Thurgood Marshall, the first African American on the Supreme Court. He had argued the *Brown v. the Board of Education* case that struck down the concept of "separate but equal" education. I read *Great Expectations* by Charles Dickens, *The Wealth of Nations* by Adam Smith. I went crazy for Russian novels like *The Brothers Karamazov* by Dostoevsky. The prison library was only okay, but the librarian was tremendous; if you wanted anything the library didn't have, she'd work hard to get it through inter-library loan. I began taking classes, anything that was offered. I started tutoring a GED class and discovered that I loved to teach. One day a young kid from Laos told me, "Andres, when you explain things, I understand them perfectly. I feel like I can do anything." That made me feel so good, so *powerful.*

For the first time, I was beginning to form a vision of my future—something beyond making some cash, or going to a club, or meeting a girl. I began to believe I could play a positive role in the lives of others. I was developing the ability to think of myself in the third person, to look at myself and think, "Here's this kid—Andres—on a journey. What will he do? How will his story turn out?"

An incident that happened about then had a profound influence on me. One night I was watching the Spanish-language news program *Primer Impacto*. The program showed video of a young man trying to cross the Rio Grande River between Mexico and the U.S. I watched him swimming against the strong current, growing more tired with each stroke. Eventually, he simply disappeared under the muddy surface of the water.

I sat there in my cell, deep in thought, after watching that young man drown. I thought about what might have been going through his mind as he struggled. I imagined him thinking, "If I get across, I can send money to my mother. If I get across, I can send for my kids." But he *didn't* get across, and he'd never have a chance to do anything again. I thought about my father, who had made a similar risky trip across the border to get to this country. And here I was, repaying his efforts by landing in prison. And that's a reality all of you can relate to, whether you're Latino, Black, white, Asian, or some other ethnicity. No matter who you are, there has likely been someone in your past who made tremendous sacrifices for you.

In my case, watching that young man die gave me the inspiration to work harder than I ever had before.

I committed myself to going to college. I had access to the newspaper *USA Today*, and during the month of September, it ran a series on how to apply to college. I followed the directions precisely and applied from inside a prison cell. This was close to six years in on my bid. On my second opportunity for parole, armed with an acceptance letter from the University of Rhode Island, I convinced the board to release me in time to begin school in the fall of 2004. After one semester of receiving excellent grades at URI, I was accepted at Brown University. At Brown, I narrowed my goals even more. With my larger vocabulary I was now able to articulate "what I want to be when I grow up." That goal is to be an advocate for the highest-quality education for children—for *all* children. After graduating from Brown, I began to pursue this dream by entering Yale Law School in September 2008.

Voces Latinas

If it was not too late for me when I was in prison, it is definitely not too late for you to begin turning your own life around. I do not make this claim lightly. I realize the harsh reality that many of you are living in. I know that reading a book today will not ease most of your problems. However, the fact remains that how you prepare yourself for the future will make a great difference.

Do you know the TV show *The Wire*? In that show, the characters in prison have a saying about how they will do their time, no matter how long the bid may be. They say, "When you go to prison, you only do two days: the day you go in and the day you come out." But those of us who have been in prison know that the time is filled with the in-between days. The in-between days are long; the in-between days are lonely; the in-between days are monotonous. But the in-between days are the days that will determine everything. I used my in-between days wisely and managed to turn my life around. I went from prison to an Ivy League college to the best law school in the country, if not the world. I say that not to brag, but to illustrate the power of using every day to its full potential. In the long run, this strategy will always yield great rewards.

Andres Idarraga

Wherever you find yourself, whatever your situation, you can use your days wisely. Like me, you can find a passion. Together, let us be passionate about our future by acquiring the tools and the learning we need to find work that interests us. Let us define and pursue our own goals. Let us take the initiative to create the world we want for ourselves. And when we have done all that, let us pay it forward by teaching younger generations how to do it.

I will end with a poem I came across while I was still in prison. This poem has both motivated me and haunted me ever since I first read it, and I often come back to it. It was written by Vachel Lindsay in 1914 and is titled "The Leaden-Eyed":

> Let not young souls be smothered out before
> They do quaint deeds and fully flaunt their pride.
> It is the world's one crime its babes grow dull,
> Its poor are ox-like, limp and leaden-eyed.
>
> Not that they starve; but starve so dreamlessly,
> Not that they sow, but that they seldom reap,
> Not that they serve, but have no gods to serve,
> Not that they die, but that they die like sheep.
>
> Let us fully flaunt our pride and not die like sheep.

Maria Cárdenas

About Maria Cárdenas

In her mid teens, Maria Cárdenas seemed destined to be just another sad statistic. She had endured years of physical, emotional, and sexual abuse. Forced into a loveless marriage, she was already a mother. She could barely read or write. But somehow she continued to believe that life held something more for her. With remarkable courage and determination, Maria showed the world that she was right.

Maria Cárdenas Speaks

As I was growing up, I learned what a "good woman" was. I saw that a good woman cooked her man's food from scratch, making fresh tortillas every day. She had total responsibility for her kids, and she had as many kids as she could. She worked with her husband in the fields. On Saturday and Sunday her man went out to drink while she stayed home with the kids. If she had time, she could watch the *telenovelas*. She had no desires of her own, no ambitions. She received very little respect from those around her.

Voces Latinas

This is the image of womanhood that I grew up with. This is what I was taught lay in store for me.

My parents were Mexican migrant workers. I was the second of their eight children and the oldest girl. From the time I was a toddler, I—like my siblings—worked in the fields alongside my parents. We drove back and forth across the country, staying in crowded migrant camps, spending our days picking tomatoes or cucumbers, oranges, potatoes, or beans. The sun scorched my skin while the leaves sliced my hands. Oils from the vegetables stained my nails. We kept a constant lookout for snakes hidden in the brush.

As the years went on, my father worked less and drank more, standing at the edge of the fields chatting with the *jefes* (bosses) and throwing stones at us if we didn't pick fast enough. At home he beat my mother terribly, and eventually began beating us kids as well. We attended school at times, but with our constant moves and my father's demands that we work as much as possible, I learned next to nothing. Even when we lived in one place for a while, I often had to stay home. As the oldest girl, I always had a baby to care for or a meal to prepare, clothes to wash or ironing to do.

And yet somehow, even when I was very young,

Maria Cárdenas

I felt certain that a woman's life—*my* life—could be better. How I knew that, I can't say. It was not because of anything I observed. Still, looking at the horrible lifestyle of the women around me, I thought, "My life will not be like that."

By the time I was 12, we were living apart from my father, and I was able to attend school more regularly. I desperately wanted to learn. But I was so far behind the other students that I didn't know how to catch up. When I asked questions about material I didn't understand, the teachers were impatient, and I was too shy to make a fuss. So I mostly stayed quiet, sitting like a ghost in the back of the classroom, picking up what I could.

Then when I was 14, an amazing thing happened: A teacher, a woman named Mrs. Mercer, noticed me. She asked if I wanted to work Saturdays at the western clothing store she and her husband owned. I translated for the store's Spanish-speaking customers, and I earned twenty dollars a day. That money felt like gold to me. It wasn't just the amount. It was what it told me—that I did not have to be a field worker. It told me that I could do something more.

I began to have dreams about my future. I imagined myself having a good job, an actual career. I pictured myself wearing pretty clothes and carrying a briefcase. I imagined doing something that other people respected.

The month I turned 16, Mrs. Mercer recommended me for a cashier's job at the supermarket. Six weeks later I was promoted to head cashier. That same night, the manager offered to let me go home two hours early— at 9:00 instead of 11:00. I was so excited! I could not wait to get home to tell my family the good news. But my brother couldn't pick me up until 11:00. So when a friend of his—someone I knew, someone I had worked with in the fields—came into the store and offered me a ride home, I was delighted.

What had started out as the best night of my life ended as the worst. The man didn't drive me home. He attacked me in the car, beat me, and raped me.

I don't know what your family would say if you showed up at home bruised and bloody and crying, saying you had been raped. I hope it would not be what I heard. When you live in a world like mine, where women have no status and no rights, there is no such thing as rape. I had gotten into the car with the man, hadn't I? I had "let him" do what he had done, hadn't I? What had happened had to be my fault. He, the rapist, was just being a man. I had failed to be a good woman.

When I learned I was pregnant, I truly thought

my life was over. I could see nothing ahead of me but the same life my mother had lived. The only path open to me, it seemed, was to do what my family wanted. I quit school, married the man who had raped me, and moved with him to Oklahoma. To do otherwise would have disgraced the family.

The years in Oklahoma were a nightmare. My little daughter Antonietta was the only bright spot in a life of poverty, shame, and abuse. As the days dragged on, I thought more and more about her. In spite of my saying "My life will not be like that," my life *was* like that. And what was my little girl learning about being a woman? She was learning what I had learned—that a woman has no rights, no self-respect, no ambition, and no hope.

I gathered my courage, and I left. I took Antonietta and a few belongings, and returned to Florida. My husband mocked me as I drove away. "You'll be on welfare! You'll never make it!" he said. But he was wrong. I got a divorce. I worked in the fields and in the supermarket; I kept up the payments on my little car, and I lived in peace with my daughter. I was very, very happy.

As I rebuilt my life, I realized what my next big challenge would be. Antonietta was going to school and loving it. She brought her little books home so I could read her stories. My reading skills were very poor. I knew that before long, she would hand me a book that was too difficult for me.

That was the beginning of my journey to educate myself. I won't go into all the details here. I'll just tell you that after teaching myself to read, I enrolled in a federal program that helped seasonal farm workers go to college. I took developmental courses to prepare me to start working on a degree at Edison Community College. I earned my bachelor's degree from Florida Gulf Coast University. Today I am an elementary teacher, the first Hispanic teacher ever hired by my school. Most of my students are Hispanic as well, many of them children of migrant workers. I love my job and my students so much that there are hardly words to tell you. It means the world to me to tell those little children, "Yes, I grew up like you. But now I am a college graduate and a teacher. You can do that, too."

Now I want to talk about another very important chapter in my life. That is my marriage to my husband, Alfonso. I met and married Alfonso after I moved back to Florida. Together we raised Antonietta, who is a lawyer today, and we have two more children—Korak, who is in college, and Jasmin, a high-school senior. It has been so important to me to have a husband who is supportive of me achieving my goals. Believe me, during all those years of me going to school and now teaching, there have been plenty of times I failed the "good woman" test! But Alfonso has always been patient and understanding, and I so much appreciate that about him.

But I want you to understand something. Yes, I am fortunate to have a good man like Alfonso in my life. But it was not just a matter of luck. From our first days together, I told Alfonso that getting an education and having a career were things I was determined to do. I was not going to stay home and be a traditional Hispanic wife and mother. "If that bothers you," I told him, "we should say goodbye." I could see that Alfonso understood, and that my goals were truly important to him.

My point is this: If you have dreams and ambitions, it's not enough to just hope that your man will support them. If you get involved with someone hoping that eventually you can change him, chances are you will see your dreams shrivel up and die. When I was in college, I saw a Hispanic woman whose husband left her because going to school didn't fit his image of what his wife should be. I've seen other women start school and drop out because their husbands weren't supportive. Please, when you are considering choosing a man to spend your life with, think about these things.

It's hard enough even with a supportive man. In my own family, I continue to feel like an outsider. People were horrified when I went back to school. I was called selfish and strange, and a bad wife and mother. "What is she—crazy?" people asked. The whole family used to come to my house, and I'd cook and they'd all enjoy themselves. I rarely have time to do that now, and that doesn't sit well with them. Many of them have grown distant. "She's too good for us now," they say. "She's snooty. She associates more with Anglos than with us."

I'm sorry they feel that way. It would be nice to have my family's understanding and support. But you know what? It's okay. As long as I have the support of my husband and my kids, I am fine. And my job—I honestly cannot tell you how wonderful it is. Every day is a joy. When the dismissal bell rings, I am always surprised that it's already time to go home. Imagine— the shy little migrant girl, barely literate, scared and abused, is now Mrs. Cárdenas, the teacher. And yes, I wear pretty clothes and carry a briefcase!

The best thing of all? When I teach an eight-year-old girl who has to go home to make the tortillas, I think, *That was me.* I know why she doesn't have her schoolwork done. It's because she's been caring for her baby brother and helping her mother cook. I can help that child. I won't be like those impatient teachers who ignored me as I sat in the back of the room. I can help that little girl come up with her own definition of a "good woman." She can grow up knowing, as I know now, that dreams really can come true.

Angel Cordero

About Angel Cordero

Angel Cordero's hometown of Camden, New Jersey, is well known for all the wrong reasons. The city has the highest poverty rate in the nation. Unemployment is high. The FBI ranks it as one of the country's most dangerous cities. Few students finish high school, and even fewer go on to college. Angel grew up in Camden and followed what is, sadly, a typical Camden kid's path: dropping out of school, getting involved in crime, becoming dependent upon drugs, and going to prison. Yet along the way, Angel developed a vision of a different Camden—a Camden where children could safely go to school and receive a solid education. This is the story of how he has tried to make that vision a reality.

Angel Cordero Speaks

In high school, I was a good wrestler. Actually, I was a *great* wrestler. I made All-American twice, went to the regionals, all that. Wrestling was going to be my ticket out of Camden. I couldn't read, but I figured wrestling would still get me a scholarship and I'd figure things out from there.

But that didn't work out. The summer after my tenth-grade year, I stopped by my high school, Woodrow Wilson, and found out they were scrapping the wrestling program. They were eliminating it and adding *golf*. Golf! What were they thinking? Tiger Woods wasn't even born yet. Nobody I knew played golf. So I got myself transferred to Camden High School, which still had a wrestling program. The coach there was delighted to have me. And then one day when I was working out, the principal walked through. She tapped me on the shoulder and said, "You can't come here just for wrestling. Get out."

That was my last day in school. I walked out and found a job on a used car lot. Then things went bad. Well, not at first. I was a good salesman. All you need to sell cars is a good mouth, and I can talk. My boss knew I couldn't read, but he liked me anyway. He made me a manager. I hired some relatives to work there. Then some money got stolen, and I didn't tell my boss. Instead, I covered it up. I told the people involved, "You've got to return the money." But it didn't get returned, and I kept cooking the books. Things got worse and worse. I started selling drugs to get back the missing money, and soon I was in trouble with the law. After my second conviction, while I was out on bail, I ran. I left New Jersey and ran to Florida.

In Florida I started going to a gym to box. I got noticed by Michael Bell, a great kickboxer—a champion. He started training me. It was wonderful, but I knew that if I started to fight I'd draw attention and the police would be there. And I was homesick anyway, so I went back up north. I never told Mike Bell I was running; I just left with no explanation. I've always felt bad about that.

Back home, I went to work at a car wash in Philly, doing detailing. I was a crack addict, living on the street. The way the drug affected me, I'd have seizures all the time. Once I fell into the street, my face straight into the gravel. So that's how things were when the FBI showed up. I went to prison for three years.

In prison I met the nicest people. I'm not kidding. A lot of them were just great. But you know what we had in common? Almost all of us? We were uneducated. Most of us couldn't even read. In a nutshell, that's why we were there. In this country, if you are uneducated, you will fail. Chances are you will end up in jail. Maybe you'll commit a crime. Or maybe it'll happen like this: Your mom will send you to the corner store. There's drug dealing going on there, and you'll be in the store when a raid goes down. You're just standing there, but you're a Hispanic kid, so you'll get picked up, too. In court, you'll be told the only way to get out of there is to accept a plea bargain, even if you didn't do anything. This happens every day in Camden. It can happen because uneducated people are powerless. They can be treated like animals.

In jail, I had time to think about these things. I tried to earn my GED, but I failed twice. I did learn to read though. When I got out of jail, I went back to work at the used car place. I couldn't stop talking to my friends about what we could do to save our community.

I was obsessed by what I saw around me. Our kids went to school to be threatened and beaten. Our old people didn't dare go out after dark for fear they'd be mugged. A few of us started the Coamo Social Club, named after a city in Puerto Rico. The club was a place for people to come together to see what we could do to change things.

I was beginning to think like an activist. We got involved with the mayor at the time, Milton Milan. Milton ended up going to prison on corruption charges. But he was still the best mayor Camden ever had. He put the drug dealers in prison; the killings went way down. He lit a spark in people that had not been lit before. He made them realize they could take back power rather than just passively accept the idea that Camden is hopeless.

I was all over the place. I was involved in immigration rights marches, in filing suits against the Camden school district, in protesting police brutality, whatever. I was constantly going to the office of our assemblywoman, Nilsa Cruz-Perez, talking about the schools. Every day, it became clearer to me that education is the one thing we can give our kids that cannot be taken away. So when Dan Gaby, the executive director of something called Excellent Education for Everyone—we call it E3 for short—told her he was looking for a regional coordinator, she had me in her office in ten minutes flat. She would have done anything to get rid of me at that point. The next day, I was on a plane to Milwaukee to start training. There, I saw kids—the same kind of kids we have in Camden— basically educating themselves, with the involvement of their whole families. It was the most beautiful thing I'd ever seen. I was crying the whole time I was there, crying tears of frustration. I kept thinking, "If they can do this in Milwaukee, why can't we do it in my city?"

I've now been employed by E3 for seven years. E3 is a coalition of people working to bring school choice to everyone. The conditions in Camden Public

Schools are horrendous. The dropout rate is something close to 80 percent. The schools are like zoos, like prisons. People are afraid to send their kids there. And nothing changes, because the families have no choice. If the parents had the option of sending their children somewhere else, they'd have leverage. As it is, the schools know the parents can't do anything, so there isn't any pressure to change things. E3 is working to give choices to poor parents. For instance, we now have a bill before the New Jersey state legislature that would make available $9,000 for every high-school student and $6,000 for every elementary and middle-school student, so that they can attend any school they want.

While I worked for E3, I continued my other activist work. At one time, I was working on a recall petition for the Camden mayor, collecting signatures. I was taking heat because she was African American, and some people accused me of going after her because she was Black. In the middle of all that, on December 20, 2006, fifteen families came to me and said, "Angel, you have to help. The violence in the schools is so critical. If we don't send our kids to school, we can go to jail. But we can't go on risking their lives. We can't send them there anymore. What can we do?"

Angel Cordero

Just days after that, a huge Black man with a huge voice came to my office and said he wanted to talk with me. I said, "Great, you want to join the recall effort?" He said no, but he wanted to have lunch with me.

We went out and talked for three hours. He was Tim Merrill, co-pastor of Bethel United Methodist Church. We talked about the recall, and I told him the problem wasn't a racial thing; the problem was that the mayor wasn't doing her job, in my opinion. I learned about him, how for all his life he'd been taking kids off street corners, tutoring them, getting them literacy training, helping them get jobs, doing whatever he could. Then I told him about the fifteen families who had asked me for help, and Tim said, "Let's homeschool them." I said, "Where?" He said, "At my church." You know what I learned that day? That there are many messiahs in the world, and Tim is one of them. He saves kids.

I was up to my neck in working on the recall. But I knew I couldn't continue that effort and do what this man was suggesting. I thought about it for thirty seconds, and I canceled the recall. A lot of people were angry with me, and a lot of others laughed at me. But I knew for certain that this was what I had to do. I had to focus on the kids.

We met with the fifteen families at a hair salon across the street from Woodrow Wilson High School, and we talked about homeschooling, an idea that was brand new to all of them. On January 3, 2007, we started classes at the church. It was Tim, me, and my secretary. We expected fifteen kids; twenty-seven showed up. The church provided fifteen laptop computers. Three weeks after we opened our doors, someone broke in and stole the computers. But we kept going, and six months later, we graduated fourteen kids. And they're all doing well, every one of them. All are in college, helping in their parents' business, in the Army, or in trade school. We held the graduation at the Camden City Hall, and it was truly a joyous celebration.

Now we have 105 kids, with one or two more showing up every day. Eighty-nine percent are Hispanic. We have five teachers, more or less. Two are paid for by a benefactor; the rest are volunteers. The only qualification for a kid to come here is that he or she wants to. One judge tried to send a kid here by force. I said, "No way." Just as I tell the kids here, "If the day ever comes when I have to hire a security guard to keep peace, I'll dismantle the program. That is not what we are about here."

We're not giving them the greatest education. We

know that. We have them for maybe six months, after the public schools have had them for eight or ten years. But we are doing all we can. We take them on field trips twice a month—to the statehouse, to superior court—so they can see how their government works and *doesn't* work. We took them to see the movie *The Great Debaters*, about an outstanding debate team from a small Black college. We work on multiplication tables and vocabulary and current events. We are constantly looking for opportunities for them, like the tech school I just learned about that trains people to do medical billing. After an eight-week course, the graduate can earn from $13 to $17 an hour. That's an opportunity to be seized.

We're just scraping along as best we can. But we have love and respect for these kids. And when kids feel loved and respected, you can reach through that invisible wall that's around them. They're my dogs, every one of them. I am so proud of them for being here and for wanting more out of life.

The Department of Education doesn't want to deal with us. They say, "Oh, we have plans. You'll see real progress in five years, ten years, fifteen years." But I can't wait fifteen years. I have kids who need help *today*. They have been let down by every adult in their lives, and I tell them that Pastor Tim and I will not let them down.

I love these kids. And I don't want what happened to me to happen to a single one of them. Once you are stained by the judicial system, you are marked for life. No matter what I do, somebody will always say, "Yeah, but you know he's an ex-con." Education will make the difference in these kids' lives. I am going to do everything in my power to see that they get it.

Lupe Valdez

About Lupe Valdez

In 2004, Lupe Valdez made history by becoming the first elected female sheriff in the state of Texas. In 2008, she was re-elected to her post as sheriff of Dallas County. Lupe's election made headlines not only because of her gender but also because she was the first Hispanic sheriff of Dallas—as well as being a Democrat in a largely Republican county. To make her election even more remarkable, she is open about being a lesbian. This child of Mexican-American migrant workers tells her story here.

Lupe Valdez Speaks

I'm the youngest of seven children. It was as if we had two separate families: my parents had five children, then there was a gap of eleven years, and then they had two more children. Our home was in San Antonio, Texas, but because we were migrant workers we traveled constantly. We'd follow the crops as far north as Michigan—picking green beans, corn, beets, and sweet potatoes. But as the two youngest children reached school age, Mom put her foot down and said, "We're not going anymore. The last two will go to school." At first Dad said, "Fine, then we [he and the boys] will go without you." He left with the older children, while my brother Ramiro and I remained in San Antonio to go to school. But Dad returned in a month and took a job as a laborer with the city, because he could not handle everything that needed to be done. Living in one place permanently made a big difference. We, the two youngest children, eventually went on to college and graduate school. My older siblings didn't get to go to school. They all did all right, as they are hard workers. But most of them can't read very well.

When I was a child, San Antonio was very much a segregated town. There were three areas: the Hispanic area, the Black area, and the Anglo area. We lived in the *barrio*. At home we spoke only Spanish. At school, though, we were told that people who spoke only Spanish were second-class citizens, so I tried hard to speak English. Then when I was in junior high, a teacher took me aside and said, "Lupe, you ought to go to college. But you won't get in if you stay in school in this area. You need to go to a school that prepares people for college. Here are the names of some good schools across town. You need to go to one of them."

I honestly do not know why he singled me out. I don't think I was an outstanding student. But I made

A's and B's, and I wasn't in a gang or anything like that. I didn't waste time. I just did what I was supposed to do.

When I told my parents I wanted to change schools, my dad hit the roof. Looking back, I can understand why. As I mentioned, San Antonio was strictly segregated at that time. If you were caught in the wrong area after dark, the police were likely to beat you up. They'd say, "We'll teach you to stay where you belong." Several times Dad and my brothers had been caught literally "on the wrong side of the tracks" and had been badly beaten. So when I told Dad I wanted to go "over there" to school, his response was "Absolutely not. I will not let you." Because "over there," you see, he couldn't protect me.

So the fighting started. Night after night we fought, screamed, argued. We made the windows shake with our fighting. It was the beginning of many arguments between my dad and me. He was determined that I would obey, but I was unbelievably stubborn. My niece tells me that on one occasion she hid in a closet and watched us fight. My dad whipped me, and I just stood there taking it, not flinching. When he stopped, I said, "Is that all you've got? You can't hit any harder than that?" He walked away. Later, at my dad's funeral, my brothers told me that Dad would say to them, "I just *cannot* make that girl do what I want her to do!" I'm sure it was hard for him, as macho as he was, to have a daughter defy him as I did.

So I went to the school on the other side of town—an Anglo school—and to get there I rode a public bus. It was like traveling into a different world. When it rained, I noticed that I was one of the few at school with muddy shoes. I wondered how those white kids kept their shoes clean when it was rainy. Then I realized that the streets in the white part of town were paved. On our side they were dirt.

Socially, school was not great, but not awful. People were polite. I had to leave as soon as classes were done in order to get the bus back home, so I couldn't be involved in after-school clubs or sports. Academically, the students were far ahead of me. I'd frequently hear teachers make offhand comments such as "I know you already understand this, so I'll just move ahead. . . ." and I'd be sitting there thinking, "What?" The other students *did* understand, but I did not. I never objected. I just sat there quietly doing the best I could. But I was learning that the concept of "separate but equal" education was a joke.

Fortunately, a teacher who had previously taught

in the *barrio* figured out what I was experiencing. She said, "If you want to come to school early, I'll help you." So I'd arrive early and go to her classroom, and she'd explain things. Naturally, I didn't have any help with homework at home. My parents didn't read English. And the tension continued about me going "over there." When I got home, I'd hear "Do your chores." I'd say, "I need to study." They'd say, "That's your problem; you wanted to go to that school. Get your chores done."

As hard as it was, everything that happened made me more determined to stick it out. I'd bring notes home that said, "Lupe needs 15 cents for a notebook" or "Lupe needs 75 cents for a gym uniform," and there would be a family crisis. The conviction grew in me that life should not have to be such an endless struggle, and that education was the key to something better. No one should have to fight over a 15-cent notebook. You shouldn't have to scrimp on food in order to get a gym uniform. Somehow my heart kept telling me, "There has to be something better than this."

The district superintendent of the Nazarene church we attended came to our house to speak to my parents concerning my going to college. "You should let Lupe go to a Nazarene college," he said.

Dad said, "Absolutely not. We don't have the money." The superintendent said, "She can work." As soon as I found that out, I continued to beg my father for permission to go. It came down to Dad saying, "You will not attend college while you're under my roof." So instead of going to school in Texas, I left home and went to Bethany Nazarene College in Oklahoma. There was no financial aid in those days, so when I arrived, I said, "I have no money. What can I do?" I went to work in the school cafeteria.

At first it was very, very, very rough. There was so much I didn't know. My math was bad; my reading skills were atrocious. I had to study twice as hard as other people, even though I had less time because I was putting in so many hours at work. One semester I was on academic disqualification and went home to work. Even then, I took classes at San Antonio Junior College so as not to lose my momentum. When I returned, I majored in business. I didn't have a clear idea what I wanted to do, but I knew I needed to make money, so being a businesswoman of some sort sounded good.

After college, I applied for a low-level government job in San Antonio. The other four candidates were Anglos. We all took the required civil service exam, and I scored the highest. I said to the secretary administering the test, "So that means I get the job, right?" Her eyes filled with tears and she said, "If I hired you, I'd be fired." She would not be allowed to hire a Hispanic person. When I heard that, I knew I could not live in San Antonio. I moved to Kansas City to live with college friends, and I worked as a substitute teacher. I ended up joining the Army Reserve, and I spent thirteen years there, moving up to the rank of captain in a tank battalion. After basic training, I became a correctional officer at the local prison. Later I applied to become a federal agent. Dad really had problems with that. "You'll become like all the other cops," he said. "You'll beat up Hispanics."

I really loved being an agent. I worked in anti-drug efforts throughout South America, doing training with local law enforcement. But it was not always easy. As a female *and* a minority, I was very much a rarity. One time I attended a training session on working undercover. I was the only woman there. The trainer was an agency big shot from Washington, D.C. This was at the time when females were starting to take management roles in law enforcement. During a break, I went to the bathroom and came back to find a crowd of agents, many of whom were good friends of mine, clustered around this guy. As I walked up, he said loudly, ". . . and I'll be blankety-blanked if I'll ever take orders from someone who has to sit down to pee."

The other agents glanced around at me. Nobody knew what to do. From the roots of my hair to the tips of my toes, I felt tears welling up. I wanted to cry, but I was damned if I would cry in front of that man. I swore to myself, though, that if I ever got to be in management, I would never make *anyone* feel the way I felt that day. I have tried hard to honor that promise.

I am glad to say that before the end of his life, Dad was able to come to terms with my profession. At one point, I was in San Antonio to testify in a trial. I called my parents and arranged to visit them at the senior center where they liked to have lunch with the other *viejecitos.* When I walked in, Dad said, "Do you have your badge with you?" I said, "Of course," and indicated it was in my pocket. He took me from table to table, proudly introducing me, saying, "Look, this is my daughter! She's a cop, but she doesn't beat people up. Sometimes she even stops other cops from beating people." And he reached in my pocket and pulled out my badge to show them. That was a great day, because it was clear that some healing had happened between us.

People sometimes ask, "How did your parents

react to you being a lesbian?" The answer is a little complicated. I didn't come out until I was in my 30s. Actually it took me a long time to come out to *myself*, let alone to other people. I knew as I was growing up that I was different. For instance, when my friends and I would see movies, they'd identify with the girl getting rescued by the guy. *I'd* identify with the guy. And in college, there were girls I had strong feelings for, but I told myself that it was just friendship. But after college when I was living in Kansas City, I went to talk to a therapist. She said, "Well, you know what this is, don't you? You're a lesbian." My immediate response was, "No, no; that can't be." I fought the idea; I didn't want to accept it.

At her suggestion, I got involved with groups that brought gay and straight people together to work on issues of social justice. I met other lesbians and saw that they were normal, decent people.

But I still struggled for years. My spirituality has always been very important to me. And I'd been taught that you could not be in the right relationship with God and be homosexual. During this time, when I got home from work I'd go running. I'd run for miles and miles, praying all the time, begging God to take this thing away from me.

Eventually I went to Metropolitan Community Church, a church that has a special outreach to the gay and lesbian community. The first time was on Easter Sunday. I arrived late because, probably like every other person going there for the first time, I drove around the block several times before I got up the courage to stop. The church was packed; the only empty seats were in the front. I sat down and looked around me. In front of me were two men with their twin six-year-old girls, the little girls dressed in their Easter finery. When time came for Communion, the congregation took it row by row. The men and the little girls went forward and knelt down as the pastor prayed over them. Looking at this family, these ordinary nice men and their sweet little daughters, I felt emotional. I said, under my breath but obviously loud enough for someone to hear me, "Oh my God, where have you been?" And the woman standing in front of me turned and said, "We've been right here, waiting for you."

After that day I had many long talks with the pastor, and I came to believe—I came to *know*—that I could be in the spirit of God and still be who I am, a lesbian.

And so what did my parents think? Well, gradually I started bringing my partners home for Christmas.

Lupe Valdez

My parents always loved them. The women I had relationships with were always good people, nice people, and everyone got along great. But we never discussed the subject.

When I decided to run for sheriff, I went to several local officials to ask for their support. One of them gave me excellent advice. She said, "Don't lie about who you are. On the other hand, don't let the fact that you're a lesbian be the first thing the voters learn about you. Push it back." And I did. The local gay newspaper tried to out me several times, but I would not be rushed. I wanted the public to fully understand my experience, my education, my qualifications, before they were distracted by any other issue. I had twenty years of experience in law enforcement: I'd worked in the local prisons; I'd been a captain in the military; I'd been a federal agent; I'd worked in overseas anti-drug efforts. I got all that out in the public eye. And then when my opponent outed me, I didn't deny it.

It was a very, very close election. I won by only 2 percent. But you have to realize that Dallas County is historically very conservative. I'm not only the first *woman* sheriff—in fact, the only elected woman sheriff in Texas—but I'm Dallas's first *Hispanic* sheriff. Add to that the facts that I'm a Democrat and openly lesbian—and yes, a lot of people thought my winning was unlikely.

Now I've been elected to my second term. It was an even uglier campaign than the first; they threw everything they could think of at me. And still I won that election by 10 percent. I am so proud of the people of Dallas for seeing through the smear tactics and voting on the basis of my record.

I'm also very proud of the things we've accomplished here. One of the things I feel best about is the way we've opened up the department to minorities. When I first came into office, I asked, "How do we handle promotions here?" I was told, "Well, Sheriff, just say who you want promoted, and that person will pass the test." That's how it had always been done. I said, "No, no, no! We're not going to do it like that anymore." I brought in an outside vendor to test the people applying for promotions. The testing was blind; in other words, the people scoring the tests didn't know an applicant's name or race or gender. People were promoted purely on the basis of their scores. And you know what? Minority promotions went up 27 percent. Now maybe I'm wrong, but I don't think the minority employees suddenly got a lot smarter than they'd been before. Something else had been going on.

Lupe Valdez

On the other hand, not all minorities are happy with me. When I came into office, a group of Latino officers came to see me, saying, "Okay, this is what we want from you." What they were demanding was, basically, unfair privileges for themselves. I said, "So you want me to replace the good old boys network with the good old *vatos* network?" Taking orders from a Latino female has not been easy for some people to handle.

And I get stacks of hate mail, particularly from the religious right, saying things like "You should kill yourself; maybe then God would be able to forgive you" or "What a disgrace to have someone like you in office." But I didn't take this job thinking it would be easy.

What makes everything worthwhile is stories like this one:

As sheriff, when I'm invited to attend a social function, I generally take someone from the department along. If the function is given by a particular group— Latino, African American, Asian, Jewish, Muslim, whatever—I try to find a representative of that group from my department to go with me. Recently when I was invited to speak to an Asian community organization, I asked a young Asian deputy to come along. He was great. He is a good-looking young man; he spoke the language, and he charmed everybody. As I was leaving the banquet, he said, "Oh, Sheriff, before you go . . ." and I thought, "Oh crap, he's going to ask for some special favor." But he said, "I just wanted to say that I know if it weren't for you, I wouldn't have had the opportunity to be a deputy. A lot of us know that. So I just wanted to say thanks."

Why did I run for sheriff? Shoot, for moments like that! In ten years I'll be long gone, but that young man and others like him will still be here. They'll be making the department a better place. Together we're in a position not to give preferential treatment to minorities but to put standards of fairness and equality in place for *everyone*. I feel terrific about being part of that.

Bobby Rodriguez

About Bobby Rodriguez

Much is said and written about teenage mothers—the problems they face and the difficulties their children have to deal with. What people often forget is that for most teenage mothers, there is a teenage father as well. Bobby Rodriguez was a teen father. Today Bobby is an insurance consultant with a stable home. But he can't forget that his oldest child was born to a father who had not yet grown up himself. Here, Bobby talks about his changing perspective on what it means to be a father.

Bobby Rodriguez Speaks

I lived in Brooklyn until I was 13, in a very diverse area. The Italians were on 4th Avenue between 7th and 10th; the Hispanics were on 7th between 5th and 6th. There were also the Black section and the white section, with everybody defending their territory. And there was intra-group tension, too; the Hispanics from Park Slope didn't like the Hispanics from Red Hook, stuff like that. People who grew up there had to know how to survive.

Voces Latinas

We left New York to get away from my stepfather. Paul was a Vietnam vet with some serious issues. As a parent he was pretty rough, but the physical abuse was mostly directed toward my mom. A couple of times when he was hitting her, I tried to interfere. Once I threw a chair at him, and another time I grabbed a belt and jumped on his back and tried to choke him. Those times I got tossed around pretty good.

Eventually, my mother's sisters, who lived in Pennsylvania, convinced her to move there. An uncle pulled up with a U-Haul, and we ran for it. It was me, my older brother Billy, my younger sister Debbie Ann, and Mom. Mom actually had an older son who had been born when she was very young; he'd been raised by my grandmother. My father was in Puerto Rico.

In Pennsylvania, we stayed for a while in the town of Bethlehem, where my aunt lived. There I encountered a group of guys, almost like a gang, racially diverse. At first they wanted to fight me, but my cousin was like, "Yo, he's my cousin. He just moved here from New York. Be cool," and they embraced me. That seemed like a good thing at the time, but as it turned out, it wasn't really good. They were troublemakers.

Soon we left Bethlehem and moved to Hellertown,

Bobby Rodriguez

Pennsylvania. Talk about culture shock! The principal had warned my mother. He'd said, "You *do* realize that your children will be the only Hispanics in the school, right?" It wasn't a big deal for my sister and brother. Debbie Ann was in elementary school, and Billy was in vo-tech, but I was 13 and in middle school, and let me tell you, it was rough. There was racial hostility, lots of it. As soon as I stepped in there, I started hearing "Here comes the pork chop" or "Spic." You want to hear something ignorant? They called me "Reggie Jackson." They couldn't even get the ethnic group right. They could at least have said "Chi Chi Rodriguez"—he's Puerto Rican—but no, it was Reggie Jackson, an African American.

I knew Mom wanted to make a fresh start in Pennsylvania, so I really tried to keep my nose clean, but eventually I started retaliating. I'd walk in and hear "Hey, spic." I'd go over to the group and say, "Who said it?" and the kid who thought he was toughest would say, "*I* said it," and we'd go at it until we both got hauled off to the principal's office. Generally the other kid got suspended; the principal knew what was going on. Only once did I really get in trouble. Here's what happened: When I went to use the restroom, there was a line. I stood there, waiting until I was next, but the guy in back of me said, "Hey, pork chop, get to the back." I said, "I don't think so." He blocked me with his arm and stepped in front of me. I said, "Yeah, okay, you go ahead." But when he did, I followed him into the stall and pissed on his leg. *Ay yi yi*—what a scene there was then! We were duking it out, kids were screaming, teachers were running in, and we were dragged to the principal's office with this big wet stain on the other guy's pants. That time I was suspended; the principal said pissing on his leg was unnecessary.

I was a very good student. I went to school seriously, to study. I really had a vision of my future. I'd always been fascinated by planes, and I wanted to join the Air Force and eventually become a commercial pilot. But after a year in Hellertown, Mom got a place in a new apartment complex back in Bethlehem, where we'd stayed originally, and we moved. Mom thought, "Oh, it's a more diverse community; Bobby won't have these problems anymore," when really my problems were just beginning.

When I began high school in Bethlehem, I hooked up with the group of guys I'd met there earlier, and everything started—drugs, alcohol, stealing. Using coke, even crack. It's strange how you can have a genuine vision of your future—and I really did, that's not just BS—and yet if you allow yourself to get involved with certain people, if you bring in alcohol and drugs, if you get involved in sex, then poof, you forget everything else. You're finding fun and satisfaction in the moment, and thoughts of the future go out the window. Before long, that vision slips so far away that you forget you ever had it.

I met Yvonne when I was in ninth grade. We started going out, but secretly. Her parents were very strict, so everything was behind their backs. Yvonne and I would skip school and go to my mom's place, and you can guess what eventually happened. We were together through high school, right through her graduation. Me—I didn't graduate. I did so poorly that I was held back twice, and finally I dropped out.

Yvonne graduated from high school in June, and our son Rafael was born in November. When I learned she was pregnant, I was really happy. I stopped using drugs. I wasn't one of those guys who says, "It's not my kid," or turns his back on the girl. We lived with my mother, and I was like Mr. Mom. I got a job at St. Luke's Hospital, working 5:00 a.m. to 2:30 p.m. I had no transportation, so I'd get up for the 3:30 a.m. baby shift and feed Rafael and change him and put him back to bed. Then I'd walk to work in the dark. It took an hour, and this was in November, so we're talking rain and snow. Yvonne worked 3:00 to 11:00 p.m., so when I got home it was all about the baby. And I was happy about it, really. I thought, "Yeah, cool. We have our little family."

After five months we moved into our own place closer to the hospital, and everything started up again— the drugs, the partying. It was so great to have my own place! I was 18, and I could have all my buddies over. My friends loved Rafael. They'd sit him up and play-fight with him, and talk about how he was going to get down with us someday. I began selling for extra money. We'd hook the baby up with fresh sneakers, little outfits. Hey, I was living the lavish life of a drug dealer, so my son should too, right? He was less than a year old, and he already had him some bling—a little gold bracelet, a gold chain.

I worked at St. Luke's for a year and a half. I cleaned the fryers and ovens in the kitchen, that kind of thing. Then the guy who scrubbed the pots and pans went on vacation, and they told me to do his job. When I said I wouldn't, they said I had to, and I walked out. I thought, "I don't need this job. I'm selling." Around that time, my brother asked if I wanted to take over the payments on his two-year-old Dodge, because he wanted to get a newer one. I thought, "Sure, I'm making money; I want a car." So now with a car, I could take off with my buddies for trips to Virginia Beach to party and get high. Sell, snort, smoke—that was my life. Sometimes I'd take a job for a little while: I sprayed lawns for a lawn-care company; I worked for a while as an assistant electrician; I loaded and unloaded trucks. But I didn't know how to keep a job. I couldn't, actually. After partying all night, I wasn't in any shape to go into work.

Things were falling apart at home. At that point, I was pretty much sitting around smoking crack all day. We'd moved again. The baby slept in the front room, and our room was in the back. Crack makes you paranoid and crazy. I became obsessed with the idea that someone was watching the house. Over and over again, at all hours, I'd go into Rafael's room and look out the window. Sometimes he'd wake up and see his strung-out father staring out there. It must have scared him. He must have thought, "What is Dad doing? Is someone going to hurt him? Is someone going to hurt me?" I'd see him watching me, and it made me ashamed. And feeling ashamed made me angry. Yvonne was very unhappy, yelling at me to quit the drugs. I became abusive. Yeah, I put my hands on her, many times. My son saw that, too. Who knows what all he saw?

One winter night my buddy and I went out in my car to buy some coke. On the way back home, we got pulled over by a state trooper. They put us into separate cruisers and took us to the station. My buddy had the coke. He was wearing long johns and had put the package in the pocket in the crotch area. When I was taken into the precinct, in handcuffs, we passed an examining room and I saw my buddy in there butt naked. I thought, "We're done." I thought about ratting out the sellers, but they were big. I knew I'd have to take the charge. I was going to prison. I'd completely blown it. I'd never be able to be a decent father now.

But the cops kept interrogating me, saying, "Where's the stuff? We know it's there. We're going to tear the car apart." Then they let me go. I couldn't understand; I *knew* they'd found it. I called my brother to pick me up, and as we were getting ready to drive away, my buddy came out. He got in the car and said, "They didn't find it." I grabbed him to beat the crap out of him. I said, "You're lying to me! Are you wired? Are you setting me up?" But it was true; somehow they'd missed checking in that pocket. They really hadn't found it.

And you know what I did then? After those moments of total terror—seeing the reality of my life, everything gone, never able to be a father to my son again? I went home and partied.

My twenty-first birthday came along. Yvonne threw a party for me. Lots of people were there. Some of them didn't know what I was up to, so instead of smoking crack in front of them I was going into the bathroom to do it. I was spraying air freshener, running the shower, all that stuff to try to cover it up. I was stoned out of my head. Eventually, my brother confronted me, saying, "What are you doing?" I went nuts and started swinging at him.

We lit into each other, fighting and screaming, and I threw him onto a glass-topped table, which broke. I was crazy, out of control. People were holding me down, sitting on me, and I started crying, thinking, "Oh God, what am I doing? This is not me; this is not me."

The worst part is that Yvonne had invited a surprise guest. Back when I was 15, I'd spent some time in Puerto Rico with my father, and I'd met this really great guy—Gilbert. He was one of those people you sometimes meet and admire; he was just such a solid, good person. And clean, man. He never did anything.

He owned his own home and had rental properties in New Jersey. He'd been so good to me in Puerto Rico, and we'd remained friends. Yvonne had called him to tell him about the party. Then when he showed up, he saw me like that.

I sat down with Gilbert and told him everything. Immediately he said, "You gotta get out of here. Come stay with me in Newark until you get straightened out." He was working as chief dispatcher for a trucking company there, and he said he'd get me a job. I said no, I couldn't leave, but he looked me in the eye and said, "You have to do this. You're going to kill yourself and ruin your family." Then he said—and I couldn't ever forget this—"Bobby, your son was watching you tonight."

I left with him that night. I stayed with him in northern New Jersey. I went through withdrawal and got sick and gradually got clean. I put in an application at his company, lying and saying I'd graduated from high school. Gilbert bought me shoes and pants and shirts and a tie, and I went to work as a dispatcher. For five months I stayed with him, just going home on weekends. Then I moved home and commuted to Newark for another seven months. I got hired by Capital Blue Cross/Blue Shield to do customer service, and I worked at that for three years. My family and I moved briefly to Florida, then back to Pennsylvania, and I returned to work for Capital. We had two more children along the way.

I was doing much better—staying clean, doing well in my career—but the relationship with Yvonne began to crumble. I guess she figured she had held things together while I was out partying and now it was her turn. But now I was older and so were the kids, and I was in a different place. I guess I'd grown up. We eventually split up. Later I met Migdalia, who had three kids of her own, and a year later we got married. We live in Allentown, Pennsylvania. I left Capital this last June after fourteen years to begin my own insurance consulting business.

I wanted to be a good father; I really did. Sometimes I would sit watching my baby son sleep and I would cry, feeling so bad, thinking, "I have to do better." But I was 18. When the phone would ring or my buddies would come around—bang, all my good intentions would fly out the window and I'd be a teenager again, wanting to enjoy my teenage life. In a world where there was just me and Yvonne and the baby, I was okay. But that was not the real world. In the real world, the phone rings and your buddy says,

"We're going out," and your girl says, "When are you coming back?" and you say, "I don't know," and she flips out and you're out the door. In the real world, you lose your job, they cut off the electricity, there are cockroaches everywhere, you worry about not being able to pay the babysitter—so you don't go to work, so you lose another job. And the child is watching all of that.

Rafael is 20 now. He had a rough time of it growing up. There were all our moves, all the instability, all the violence, all the times he looked around and saw someone smoking weed in the back yard or doing lines on the living room table. He's out there on the streets. He lives with his cousin, he doesn't work, and I have the feeling he's involved in the same things I was. I am very scared for him.

When you have a kid while you're a teenager, you're still a kid yourself. Who knows how long it will be until you clean up your act? Maybe you'll get it together when you're 26, or 28, or 30. By then the kid is half grown and you've done a lot of damage. It's not fair. It's not fair to the child or to you. It wasn't fair to Rafael. It's so much better to raise a child after you know how to live your own life.

Rosie Molinary

About Rosie Molinary

Rosie Molinary—a freelance writer, editor, author, and teacher—is a first-generation American of Puerto Rican descent. Her book *Hijas Americanas: Beauty, Body Image, and Growing Up Latina* was published in 2007. *Hijas Americanas* features interviews with hundreds of women discussing the often very different expectations for women that exist inside the Latino home and outside, in the larger American culture. In this essay, Rosie describes her own early insight into what it means to be a Latina American.

Rosie Molinary Speaks

It was one of many lunches that I, now an adult Latina, had with a group of sixth-grade Latinas at the local middle school. Once a month, I made my way down the school's hallway, balancing soda, cupcakes, and pizza, to visit with a group of girls that I had come to love like the little sisters I never had.

"What's up?" I asked them as we started settling into our seats with lunch. Sara poured Coke into red Solo cups for everyone. Sophia passed out plates and napkins while I handed out cheese and pepperoni pizza slices to each girl based on what I knew was her favorite.

My question was answered with a sigh here, a shrug there.

"Seriously," I insisted. "Nothing is up?" It was unlike them to be quiet like this, to not trip over each other with their joyful stories.

Sara looked at me, wondering whether or not to spill what was on her mind.

"I'm a little sad," she said. I pushed my hair out of my eyes so I could see her better.

"Why are you sad?" I asked in Spanish. Our lunch conversations always moved back and forth between English and Spanish. Each girl's first language was Spanish, so if what we were talking about was important or personal, we couldn't help but say it in Spanish.

"Because my boyfriend and I broke up," Sara said, sounding more like a forty-year-old woman who had lost everything than like an eleven-year-old girl with her whole life ahead of her.

"Why did you break up?" I asked. I lifted a slice of pepperoni to my mouth, stuffing my mouth so I would listen instead of talk.

"I did something that I shouldn't have done," she explained, regret in her voice.

Her regret startled me. It was an emotion so hard for me to hear from a sixth-grade girl about a boyfriend—a boyfriend she hadn't had the last time I visited the school. But there was more to the story.

"And Sara has been mean to us," said Sophia, who is kind but always honest, in a matter-of-fact way.

My head turned from Sara to Sophia. "Sara was mean to who? And how?"

And then the story tumbled out.

"So there are these three new girls, and they asked Sara to be their friend," Sophia explained. "And that was fine, but then those girls started talking about us— calling us 'illegal' and 'beaners' and 'spics.' And they said Sara was saying it about us, too." Sophia told her story without a sense of anger. She just relayed the facts as she remembered them, while the other girls looked on and nodded. Sara hung her head, ashamed.

Over the course of that school year, I had come to understand the challenges my *chiquitas* faced. Because anti-Latino attitudes were growing, the girls had come to really depend on one another. They rode the bus together, ate lunch together, and hung out together after school. No one else in the school was willing to reach out to them, and they had become one another's lifeline.

And then there was Sara, whose body was so mature that most people couldn't believe she was only eleven. While I knew that Sara was sweet and good-hearted, I also knew that she liked to be liked. And probably nothing felt better than having three new girls choose her to join them. Especially if those new girls could be Sara's ticket to eighth-grade boys. So who could expect Sara to turn down invitations from mean but popular girls who wanted her to be in their circle so that boys might notice all of them?

Sophia continued with her story, explaining how she confronted Sara about what she had been saying about the group and how, at first, Sara denied it.

Across the desk, Sara looked sad during this story. I rubbed a spot on my head that was starting to hurt. I tried to think of the right words to use with Sara. I knew that this problem with the mean girls and the eighth-grade boys would happen again unless Sara decided to do something about it. I knew this because I had once been in Sara's shoes.

It was in sixth grade that I first really noticed that I was different from the other kids in my school. I was the only Latina around—the only girl with jet black hair and a pale olive complexion—but I didn't realize this on my own.

One day after lunch, in the dark and musty hallway

of my sixth-grade building, I fumbled with my locker. I was tan from the summer, and my black hair hung over my eyes as I worked the lock back and forth. Lynn, a girl with a long and wild rat tail down her back, had the locker next to mine. As she closed her locker, she leaned into me and asked uneasily, "Are you mixed?"

I didn't understand what she meant. She reworded her question a couple of times and, finally, decided to be blunt: "Is your daddy black and your momma white?"

It was South Carolina in the mid 1980s. Race mattered as much in friendship as kindness and decency did. I explained about Puerto Rico. She stared at me, annoyed.

"You gotta be one or the other—white or black. I'm just gonna call you white 'cause you're smart."

That was it. She closed her locker, walked off happy, and later asked me to spend the night. I stared at her, astonished, when she asked, and I knew that her question was loaded with unspoken meaning. Her invitation to be her friend meant that I could not be me.

"I can't," I answered. I wanted to be seen the way that I saw myself—as a Puerto Rican girl trying to create her own way.

Voces Latinas

A few years later, the Fly Girls, a sexy dance group on a popular television comedy show, hit the scene. On it, Jennifer Lopez showed the world how Jenny from the Block could move. Rosie Perez was their choreographer. Daisy Fuentes was the face of MTV. Latinas were starting to get attention. And there I was, not the least bit sexy, with a *mamacita* at home making sure I covered all my parts and telling me I wasn't a *gringa*. But the stereotypes about Latina girls were getting out, and people used those ideas to judge me.

When I was in ninth grade, my guidance counselor called me into his office and eyed my file, which included perfect grades and high test scores. I had been the first kid in my elementary school's gifted and talented program. Surely there were no questions about my intelligence. There were, indeed, no questions— no questions allowed from me when my guidance counselor looked at me and said he wanted to remove me from Honors classes and put me only in vocational classes. Then he opened his office door and shooed me out.

Shocked, I stumbled down the hall, my red face drawing the attention of another counselor who believed in me and added me to his caseload. Years later, he encouraged me to apply to multiple colleges.

"Let's see how we can do," he smiled as I nodded. I took on the challenge, fueled by a desire to prove that first counselor wrong.

When I wasn't judged because of my ethnicity, I was denied it. In English class, a girl said that I was not Puerto Rican, because I was not like other Puerto Ricans she knew.

"What does that mean?" I asked her.

"You aren't pregnant or on drugs."

In her opinion, if I didn't have track marks, I couldn't be from the Caribbean. My face grew hot as I argued. I argued for my life, for the one thing I most definitely knew to be true about me.

In my world, being Latina didn't mean that I was having sex. It didn't mean that I did drugs. It didn't mean that I drank or skipped school or stole. It didn't mean that my family was here illegally. In my world, being Latina meant that I had a big heart. It meant loving people like family. It meant that I honored my parents, even when I disagreed with them. It meant that I worked hard for what I wanted. It meant that sometimes people accused me or judged me unfairly. It meant that I was not willing to judge or accuse others. It meant that I understood a celebration was about who you were with and not about what you received.

It meant that I was always kind and generous.

In the years after that moment in my sixth-grade hallway, people tried to steer me away from the young woman I wanted to be. Sometimes it was with drugs, sometimes it was with sex, sometimes it was with failing, sometimes it was with alcohol. But each time, I remembered that moment in the hallway.

"I can't," I said over and over again. And even when I felt lonely, I kept my eyes focused on what I could be or do instead.

Back in the classroom, Sara was frowning. Sophia had detailed every minute of Sara's bad behavior over the past month. For a minute, Sara said nothing. She seemed to be thinking about all the ways she had been tempted by an older boyfriend and the girls who wanted to be her "friends." Then she looked at the face of each girl sitting in the room. These girls had been by her side for a few years now. None of them looked mad. They just looked sad. And they looked like they still loved her.

"I am really sorry," Sara finally said.

The girls all nodded.

"We forgive you," Sophia said for all of them. They hugged each other and then sat back down.

Sara's eyes were still a little sad.

"Why are you still sad?" I asked her.

"I don't have anything to do anymore. I don't know what to do without a boyfriend," she explained.

"But of course you do," I insisted.

She looked at me, confused.

"Sara, what did you do in your free time before you had a boyfriend?"

"Hung out with these girls. Read. Drew pictures. Wandered around the neighborhood. Went to the library."

"Well, then do that," I told her. "Do those things. You don't need a boyfriend or those other girls to do what you like."

She nodded, suddenly understanding.

And I suddenly understood that each of my visits to the school was about more than pizza and cupcakes. Sara, Sophia, and the other girls were at an age where people might judge them. They were at an age where they might judge themselves. But these girls were my *chiquitas*, and I needed to remind them every day that they were their own bosses. If that moment with the rat tail girl and all the other moments afterward had taught me anything, it was that I would never leave another girl standing in a dark hallway alone.

Felipe Gutierrez

About Felipe Gutierrez

Felipe Gutierrez is a nurse practitioner employed by Scripps Mercy Hospital in San Diego, California. His path toward his chosen profession led through the Navy, where he had the opportunity to work in a military hospital. Today Felipe frequently speaks to young audiences about the growing need for Hispanic professionals in the field of health care.

Felipe Gutierrez Speaks

I was raised primarily in McAllen, Texas, by my grandmother and great-grandmother. I say "primarily" because my family dynamics were a little complicated. My mom and dad married in Texas and had my seven older siblings there, but when Mom was pregnant with me, they moved to Utah. Later they divorced, and my mom remarried and had twins. To make things easier, since there were eight of us and we lived in a one-bedroom home, Mom sent me to live with her mom back in Texas. For years, I moved back and forth between Texas and Utah.

Living with my *abuelas* was good in a lot of ways. I heard great stories about the old days in Mexico.

My great-grandmother had been born in Tampico, Mexico. She told me about the time when Pancho Villa, who was a general in the Mexican Revolution, came through their village and she cooked for him. Then she became friends with his wife and traveled with them. Although I was born and raised in the U.S., I think living with those older women helped give me insight into Mexican culture in a way I might not have had otherwise. Later in my life and career, that insight has been important to me.

My family members were not well educated. Mom grew up as a migrant worker, picking crops in the Dakotas, Michigan, and Utah. She had finished eighth grade. My dad, too, had about an eighth-grade education. He picked crops with my mom's family for a while, but then he got a job as a warehouse worker for Del Monte Foods. I did some field work as well; I remember picking cherries, onions, and potatoes in Utah.

My mom tells me that English was actually my first language, but that's not what I remember. In *abuela's* house, Spanish was all we spoke. So when I began school, I did not exactly shine academically. Reading and writing in English was difficult, and that was in the era when you got paddled at school for speaking

Spanish. Overall, school didn't seem meaningful to me. I was much more interested in getting home to play marbles or ride bikes with the kids next door.

Fortunately for me, though, my grandmother and aunt had other ideas. They began pushing me to do well in school. Although my grandma had no formal education, she had completed a program for low-income people to get their certificate as nursing assistants, and she worked as a home health aide. I would go with her sometimes to see clients, mostly elderly people who were better off than we were. Not only would she care for the people physically, but she'd also cook and clean for them. They liked her very much and would sometimes give her things, like dishes and furniture that they no longer needed. I enjoyed going with her. She wasn't just making a living; she was making a positive difference in somebody's life. I liked that. Observing her definitely gave me my first idea of becoming a nurse.

At home, I'd go to my aunt and uncle's house to study with my cousin. He was a year younger than I, but he was so smart and hard-working that he had skipped a grade and was doing homework similar to mine. His example helped me a lot. I began to think of school as important. I saw the praise that my cousin got, and I wanted some of that for myself. I didn't want to be the dummy of the family!

In junior high and high school, I was getting pretty good grades. But I had a hard time in other ways. As I moved back and forth between my grandmother's and mom's homes, I was bullied a lot. In Texas, where almost everyone I knew was Hispanic, most of the other kids were dropping out of school. I was a good student with glasses, a bit of a nerd, and a little chubby—and I got pushed around. Then in Utah, I was surrounded by blonde Mormons. *They* picked on me for being the weird Hispanic kid.

While I liked most of my high-school classes, I hated school socially. In a strange way, though, being bullied helped me concentrate on my studies. I knew that education was going to be the key to getting me out of there!

It was in high school that I developed a habit I have to this day: I look for help. I ask for help. I take advantage of any opportunity that can advance me toward my goals. I was constantly in the guidance counselors' office, talking about college. To be honest, the counselors were not all that helpful. I'd hear responses like "Well, Felipe, you don't have any money; you need to be realistic. . . ." And I'd say,

"Okay, but what *can* I do to make myself the best candidate possible?" Eventually I began hearing "Well, there is this enrichment program" or "There are these scholarships." And I followed up on all those leads. The Upward Bound program, for example, was very helpful. Upward Bound is an organization that helps prepare poor kids for college. Through Upward Bound, I was able to get free tutoring in math and science—classes I was struggling with but needed if I was going to go into the medical field.

By the time I graduated from high school, I'd already earned my certified nursing assistant (CNA) license. I went to work in a nursing home, where I helped patients with what we call ADL (Activities of Daily Living). I got patients up, showered, and dressed. This was not easy, because many of the patients used wheelchairs. Then I made the patients' beds, got them fed, sent them to rehab or therapy, and so on. I liked interacting with the patients, but I would watch the RNs who supervised us and I saw them doing more challenging work, such as giving medications, checking for bedsores, and dressing wounds. And they made more money.

Then I made what turned out to be a terrific decision for me. I joined the Navy. I was a corpsman—

what is called a "medic" elsewhere. I was stationed in Hawaii for four years. As a corpsman at a military hospital, I received amazing training in a variety of fields. I worked as an X-ray technician, a pharmacy technician, an emergency room technician, and an EMT who would go out when there was an injury on base.

Doing those different jobs really helped me decide what direction I wanted to go in my own training. I watched the MDs in action and thought, "That's cool, but do I want to spend all those years in school?" I worked in the pharmacy and thought, "Do I want to just dispense medicines?" I thought being an X-ray tech might become boring after a while. What I kept coming back to was the idea of being a nurse practitioner. That's an RN with additional training—at least a master's degree—who sees patients independently and does a lot of the tasks of a physician without having to go to school forever.

So that's what I did. After finishing my time with the Navy, I moved to California, where I enrolled in San Diego City College and earned my associate's degree in nursing and biology. It took me six years, because I was also working as an EMT in the local emergency room. Then I moved on to the University of

San Diego, which is a very expensive private school. But they had a lot of scholarship money. After my interview, the admissions people told me that because I was #1, male; #2, Hispanic; and #3, poor, they could offer me a lot of financial help. And they did.

I also joined the San Diego chapter of the National Association of Hispanic Nurses (NAHN), which helped hook me up with local and national scholarships. As always, I was not shy about telling everybody I talked to that I was looking for help. I remember representing NAHN at one conference that was sponsored by Hyundai, the car manufacturer. I was introduced to a Hyundai executive who asked me about myself, and after talking a bit I said, "I'd love to get my master's degree, but I'm not sure where the money will come from." She said, "I'm going to get you $2,000."

There is a really bittersweet story about how I managed to get through graduate school. I was taking a full course load and also working full-time at the emergency room. One of the ER nurses was a woman named Barbara Ramsey, who was a retired Navy commander. We became friends, and she and her partner, Sherry Henderson, occasionally asked me to house-sit when they were out of town. That was great, because they had a nice house with a hot tub, and I was living in a pretty ratty apartment. At work, Barbara was always saying to me, "Felipe, you look so tired! You're getting worn out! You can't work so much and go to school, too."

Then one day, Barbara and Sherry told me that they had a plan. They thought it was important that I finish my master's degree, and they didn't want me to have to work. They offered to give me $1,500 a month while I was in school, enough to support myself.

Sadly, neither of those women is still with us. Sherry died of breast cancer when she was only 56. Barbara died of lung cancer just three years later. But Barbara did live long enough to see me finish my master's degree. She was so proud and happy. I figure they were my angels on earth, and now they are my angels watching over me from heaven.

Today I am an advanced-practice nurse at Scripps Mercy Hospital in San Diego. I continue to be very active with the National Association of Hispanic Nurses. Through my job and NAHN, I frequently visit schools— especially schools with large Hispanic enrollments—to talk about careers in the health field. The first question I always hear is "Can a boy be a nurse?" And I say, "Sure, a boy can be a nurse. Why not?"

Felipe Gutierrez

But a lot of us have grown up with the idea that nurses are women. And especially in a culture where *machismo* is a big thing, there can be some extra pressure on a guy who chooses to do what might be viewed as "women's work." For me personally, I never felt that my gender was that much of an obstacle. I was very fortunate to come into nursing through the military, where a lot of very macho guys are nurses. Believe me—nobody ever calls a combat nurse a sissy. From my family I felt a little . . . well, not criticism, but just surprise and maybe some hesitation. I was asked a few times "But don't you have to be a girl?" In general, I think it's just a matter of education, of showing people that, yes, there are male nurses, and that there are male Hispanic nurses, and that's all good.

The fact is that we really, really need more Hispanics of both genders in health care. I was president of the NAHN San Diego chapter from 2004 to 2006, and the underrepresentation of Spanish-speaking people in the medical field was my main concern. As the Hispanic population of the U.S. grows, there will be an increasing need for Hispanic health professionals. Very often, Spanish-speaking people feel demeaned and ignored when they need medical care. When I see patients who don't speak English well and I speak to them in Spanish, their eyes light up. They're so relieved to be able to communicate.

And it's not only the language barrier; there are also cultural differences that need to be taken into account in the doctor's office or the hospital. I can only speak for Mexicans, since I am one, but we all know the stereotype: Mexicans don't go anywhere alone; they go by the carload. And it's often true; when a Mexican person is sick or hurt, the whole family shows up with him at the emergency room. Now, as a nurse and as someone who is accustomed to American culture, I see how inconvenient that can be. Sometimes I feel embarrassed when I hear someone groan, "Oh God; there are all those Mexicans in the waiting room, and now they want to go to the patient's room." But as a Mexican, I also understand how important it is for the patient to have his family around him.

When my great-grandmother was in the hospital, for instance, she needed us there. When she was alone, she was *sick*. But with her family there, she felt better. She couldn't understand the hospital food and wouldn't eat it, so we cooked for her at home and smuggled in what she wanted. If medical professionals just try to wave things like that away, saying, "That's wrong; that's silly; don't do that,"—well, that's not providing good health care. The more people in the medical community are culturally sensitive, the better they can deal with differences in ways that don't leave the patients feeling confused, insulted, and demeaned.

When Barbara and Sherry helped me earn my master's degree, all they asked in return was that I do what I can to help others pursue their dreams. In encouraging young people to enter the medical field, I like to think I am honoring my commitment to them. So please hear me when I say this: The demand for Hispanic health care workers is only going to grow. Providing health care is a wonderful and rewarding way to make a living. If you have an interest, don't let being a guy or Hispanic or poor make you think you can't do it. Maybe you don't have anyone in your life who knows how to give you direction or encouragement. You might have to do a lot of what I did—provide your own encouragement. There *are* people out there who will help you if you show that you're serious about wanting to succeed. For starters, contact the NAHN chapter in your area. Check out the website at **http://www.thehispanicnurses.org/**. Information and help are out there waiting for you. Go for it!